BREWING
Porters and Stouts

Sign above the door of the Beacon Hotel, brewery tap of Sarah Hughes Brewery in the Midlands of England. Such signs over pub doors were intended to show compliance with licensing laws and so were once common, but are now rare.

BREWING
Porters and Stouts

ORIGINS, HISTORY, AND 60 RECIPES FOR BREWING THEM AT HOME TODAY

TERRY FOSTER

Skyhorse Publishing

All rights reserved. No part of this book may be reproduced in any manner without the express written consent of the publisher, except in the case of brief excerpts in critical reviews or articles. All inquiries should be addressed to Skyhorse Publishing, 307 West 36th Street, 11th Floor, New York, NY 10018.

Skyhorse Publishing books may be purchased in bulk at special discounts for sales promotion, corporate gifts, fund-raising, or educational purposes. Special editions can also be created to specifications. For details, contact the Special Sales Department, Skyhorse Publishing, 307 West 36th Street, 11th Floor, New York, NY 10018 or info@skyhorsepublishing.com.

Skyhorse® and Skyhorse Publishing® are registered trademarks of Skyhorse Publishing, Inc.®, a Delaware corporation.

Visit our website at www.skyhorsepublishing.com.

10 9 8 7 6 5

Library of Congress Cataloging-in-Publication Data is available on file.

Cover design by Brian Peterson
Cover photo by CBCK-Christine/iStock/Thinkstock

Print ISBN: 978-1-62914-511-2
Ebook ISBN: 978-1-62914-884-7

Printed in China

AS ALWAYS, MY THANKS MUST GO TO MY WIFE FOR PUTTING UP with my obsession with brewing and brewing history. She encouraged me to go off and investigate brewing archives on my own in places like London, Oxford, and New Haven while she was left to her own devices. Neither did she complain about the time I spent brewing at home and at BrüRm@BAR, or at my desk beavering away writing about beer and brewing (and even fiction). Thank you, Lois!

I must also thank Jeff Browning, the brewer at BAR, who has been a good friend for many years—both for his insight into producing good beer, and his willingness to adapt some of my experiments to a commercial scale. He says he has learnt much from me, but so have I from him, and I think overall the score is even, and we are now into overtime.

CONTENTS

INTRODUCTION

MANY YEARS AGO, CHARLIE PAPAZIAN ASKED ME TO WRITE THE
first book in the Classic Styles series from Brewers Publications. That
was *Pale Ale*, and I later followed that with a similar effort on *Porter*.
This was at a time when the craft brewing revolution was still in its
early stages, and there was a limited supply of information and ingredients available to both craft and homebrewers. As always, such topics
never stand still, and I later wrote a much-expanded second edition on
pale ale. However, although I very much wanted to do so, I did not get
around to doing anything on porter until after I had retired from my
"day job" and had time to extend my historical researches.

While I was busy amassing ream upon ream of notes about porter
brewing in the past, modern craft brewing caught up with me as there
was a revolution in brewing this style of beer, as well as a huge expansion
in the range and quality of brewing ingredients available. It was soon
clear to me that there was a need to redo the porter book. But this time,
I wanted to not only include results from my research, but also include
stouts, since these are really only derivatives of the original porters.

I have started with the history of porter/stout brewing, partly
because its close ties to the Industrial Revolution in Britain is very
intriguing, but also because it is key to understanding how beer styles
developed, and because it shows us how the beers we make now have
come into being and why they are what they are. I have incorporated
as much as I can of the history of porter and stout in the United States,
the former especially having been a part of America's brewing portfolio

since 1776. Indeed, porter has been brewed here without a break right up to the present day, in contrast to England, where it actually ceased to be brewed from before the Second World War until the renascence of craft brewing there in modern times. Native porters and stouts have never received great acclaim here, largely because pale lager beers became so dominant in this country, and because Prohibition saw the demise of so many breweries, all too often along with the loss of their records.

I started brewing my own beer in Britain, just as the craft of home-brewing was beginning to be revived, then moved to the United States just as homebrewing was legalized here. I have therefore lived through two homebrewing revolutions, and of course through the great craft brewing revolution here. The quality of beer I can now produce at home, and that of those craft beers I can buy, has improved dramatically. Proudly numbered among all these new beers are many porters, stouts, and their sub-styles, and new variations on these are appearing almost daily. Therefore, it seemed that this was a good time to review these styles, their histories, and their brewing methodologies.

I hope I have done justice to the subject from the point of brewing and the possibilities available to the home and craft brewer. I also hope that I have given some insight into the history and importance of ale and porter brewing in the United States. There are still many gaps in this knowledge, and with luck, I shall have inspired some of you to try to fill these. Above all, I hope I have roused present and future brewers to further explore porter and stout and to continue to experiment and innovate in this area.

BREWING
Porters and Stouts

CHAPTER ONE

HOW IT ALL BEGAN... AND NEARLY ENDED

PORTER AND ITS ORIGINS HAVE LONG BEEN OF INTEREST TO ME and to many other craft and homebrewers. Part of the fascination is that (at least at first sight) it appears to have been the first recognizable style of beer, a style created by London commercial brewers who rode on its back into the first stage of the Industrial Revolution. It also appears to have been a style that sprang into being almost literally overnight and enjoyed great popularity for almost a hundred years, during which time the stout style evolved as a stronger version of porter. Porter gradually faded away to nothing in its place of origin, London, before undergoing a revival at the hands of the new wave of craft brewers in Britain, and more especially those of North America. I was born and educated in London and never so much as saw porter, let alone got to drink it, until I migrated to the United States.

Of course, although porter—and, to a lesser extent, stout—just about disappeared in Great Britain for a time, both beers continued to be brewed elsewhere. Stout continued to be a major product for Beamish, Guinness, and Murphy's in Ireland, where Guinness also continued to brew porter up until 1974. Stouts and porters in various forms also continued to be brewed in and around the Baltic area of Northern Europe. Perhaps more importantly, porter was still being brewed in the United States. It was first produced there in the eighteenth century, right up to the present day in the case of the Pennsylvania brewer,

Yuengling, and up until the 1970s in the Northeast. That continuity may partly explain why the new American craft brewers soon took to producing porter and stout.

But I need to explain what I mean about porter being the first recognizable beer style. It could not be so in the modern sense in its early years, since in the first half of the eighteenth century there was no way of determining things like original gravity or alcoholic strength. Also, at first it was very much a local beer, produced only in London and, in that sense, not much different from other types of beer produced elsewhere in Britain and Europe. But London was already a very large city, and its population was expanding, so the breweries there had great potential for growth. And indeed, it was the porter brewers who grew most rapidly as Britain edged towards the Industrial Revolution. So porter was recognized very early in its life as a "different" beer with a particular and distinctive character. It wasn't long before brewers in other parts of England, Scotland, Ireland, and even America attempted to reproduce "London porter," in several cases by employing brewers who had learned their trades in London porter breweries.

We know a lot about early porters, or at least we think we do. We think we know the brewing process that was used, that it was made from only one special type of malt, and how it was stored at the brewery so as to achieve the desired final flavor. Some sixty or so years after porter was first brewed, the hydrometer came into use, and we have some numbers for both original (OG) and finishing gravity (FG). Using that knowledge and later information, it is possible to estimate the OG of the first porters. Yet there are still questions to be asked about the brewing process and the malt, as we shall see below.

Although we cannot be sure, it seems likely that porter *evolved*, rather than being invented as a finished style. Part of the problem in deciding how the phenomenon came about is that there are more than a few myths surrounding porter, the most egregious of which has survived to the present day. So if my assertion that porter was a definite style is correct, then it still remains somewhat of an elusive style.

Let us look at how porter came into being and how it, and its offshoot, stout, developed. I have a mountain of material on this, and am by no means the only person to have delved into this piece of brewing history. Since this book is essentially about brewing porters and stouts, I needed to condense this history, and have chosen to do so in a fairly loose chronological manner. That means there may be some

A dilapidated pub sign and the perpetration of a myth.

The Old Blue Last pub today.

omissions of material that other brewing historians consider to be significant enough to be included. I have limited the number of references in the text for reasons of brevity, and have instead appended a list of some of my sources. Note that some of the points I make are purely of my opinion, although I have endeavored to base them on as much fact and general brewing knowledge as possible. I make no apology for this; rather, I hope I might stimulate some intriguing debates on them!

PORTER AND STOUT IN THE EIGHTEENTH CENTURY

According to the most commonly quoted story, this was the period in which porter was first brewed. Ralph Harwood, a partner in the Bell Brew House at Shoreditch in East London, was the brewer, and it first went on sale at the Old Blue Last in Shoreditch. There is still a pub of that name there, which was rebuilt in 1876, and until at least the 1990s it bore a sign outside saying, "the house where porter was first sold." The story goes that a drink called "three threads" was popular

The Dove is a gem of a pub on the Thames Riverside, a short walk from Fuller's Brewery. The sign is a rare instance in modern times of the word "Entire" on a pub façade.

at that time. It was a mixture drawn from different casks in the pub when ordered by the drinker. Subsequent stories vary as to the makeup of the mixture, but the most common components seem to have been ale, beer, and twopenny. Harwood supposedly developed a method to produce a single beer with the same flavor as the mixture, and was therefore called "Entire." It was customary then, since sparging had not yet been invented, to do two, three, and even four separate mashes of the grain, and to ferment each of the worts separately, ending up with one strong beer and two or three weaker beers. It is therefore held that Harwood coined the term Entire, because he mixed all the worts together to produce just one beer.

This version of the birth of porter actually first appeared in 1802, some 80 years after the event it recounted! The story appeared in a guidebook (*The Picture of London*, John Feltham), and used extracts from publications in 1760 and 1788 to pin down the date of porter's arrival on the scene as 1722. This story was repeated and repeated through the years by many authors, often reproducing Feltham's article verbatim. I have seen more than a few articles on the topic written in the twenty-first century, pleading the case for three threads and giving credit to Harwood for his "discovery." Unfortunately, it is just not true in any detail! The first oddity is that, despite the fact that other porter brewers, such as Truman and Whitbread, grew rapidly and made large fortunes, Harwood was not particularly successful—and the brewery, which he owned with his brother James, went bankrupt in 1747. It has been pointed out (*The Story of the Pint,* Cornell, 2005) that what little evidence does exist in favor of Harwood actually suggests that rather than Ralph, it was more likely his brother James who invented porter!

Secondly, there does not seem to be much evidence in favor of the popularity of three threads. A guidebook to pubs around central London (*A Vade Mecum for Malt Worms*, Ward, published around 1718) mentions it just once, although citing all kinds of other brews available to the "Malt Worm," including "amber," "double," "October beer," "oat ale," "Burton ale," and even "stout," among others. Thirdly, the concept of combining the worts to produce an Entire beer may have been nothing new. There is a published recipe from 1502 that cites the brewing of a "single" beer from the given grain ingredients, although it does not directly state that only one wort was produced from them. Fourthly, it seems more likely that porter simply evolved, as London brown beer brewers dealt with competition from ale brewers and those from the country. A gentleman writing under the splendid pseudonym of Obadiah Poundage (*London Chronicle*, 1760) states that the London brewers found that a well-hopped porter kept for some months (so that it became mellow) was the answer to their difficulties.

There seems to be no doubt that porter did exist in the 1720s. In particular, a Swiss visitor to London in 1726 wrote that most of the porter was drunk by the working classes and that there were a number of houses in London selling nothing but porter. At that time, much of the transporting of goods around the narrow streets of London was done manually, requiring a large body of men known as "porters." Such heavy labor would surely have made them very thirsty, so it is often supposed that they were the foremost group of the working classes who drank porter, and hence the name of the beer. This is certainly the most convincing story for the origin of the beer's name, although many writers have put forward other explanations, mostly of a bizarre nature!

An interesting book, entitled *The London and Country Brewer*, was published anonymously in several editions from 1734 up to 1759, and gave a recipe for brewing porter in the 1742 and subsequent editions, and one for "stout butt beer" in the 1737 edition. The author claims to have had experience brewing at a London brewery, but does not state which one. The recipes also do not indicate that the beer was brewed on the Entire system, but they do state that only brown malt was used in both cases. It further states that porter was about 25 percent weaker than the stout butt beer; my calculations suggest original gravities of about 1.080 (19.3°P) and 1.125 (about 29°P), respectively. Because of

Brown beers rule
1710

Porter arrives
1720–1730

First London and Country Brewer
1734

the vagueness of the recipes, these numbers should of course be treated with reservation.

Later evidence shows that the anonymous author was William Ellis, who wrote a number of other books, most of them dealing with purely agricultural matters. He admits in one of these that his experience in a London brewery was that of executor to his uncle's estate. He does not name the brewery and, given his executor duties, it is quite possible that he did not brew porter there at all. A good deal of the material in *The London and Country Brewer* consists of reports from other people, many of which make little sense to a knowledgeable brewer. His agricultural expertise is also in some doubt, as his neighbors thought his farm was the most poorly run piece of land in the area. In short, a case could be made that he was something of a dilettante, publishing information that he had picked up from other people and which he did not himself understand.

Ellis gave some conflicting accounts of how brown malt was dried, but does suggest that the grains were roasted and scorched, sometimes crusted and burnt, having been made to crack and jump during kilning. He is also adamant that porter and stout butt beer were made using only brown malt. This seems to have been accepted by other writers, and it is generally assumed that brown malt was the only grain used in porter and stout brewing, at least until the 1780s, when the hydrometer showed that brown malt gave much less extract than pale malt.

This raises some serious questions in my mind. We would not expect malt dried in this way to contain any starch-degrading enzymes, so this malt would cause problems in mashing unless all the starch had been hydrolyzed during kilning. It is difficult to be sure, since we don't have any eighteenth-century brown malt. However, there is much evidence

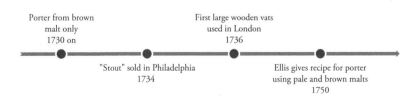

Porter from brown
malt only
1730 on

First large wooden vats
used in London
1736

"Stout" sold in Philadelphia
1734

Ellis gives recipe for porter
using pale and brown malts
1750

that it was heated rapidly while still containing some moisture, causing the grains to explode or "blow," so that it was often called "blown malt." Because of this, it was less dense than pale malt, so that the volume measure of the quarter that was used for measuring malt in those days *weighed* less for brown than pale. I have tried taking pale malt, adding a little moisture, then heating it in a variety of different ways, from a wood-fired pizza oven to a popcorn machine and through to a regular oven, but have so far failed to make it "blow." The oven drying method, without adding moisture to the pale malt, gave a result similar to modern commercially dried brown malt, and is described in the section Making Your Own Amber and Brown Malt at the end of chapter 3.

Modern commercial brown malt is not blown, and it is dried in a somewhat more gentle way than its older cousin. It does contain some starch, but has no enzymes, so it must be mashed along with pale malt to ensure conversion. We do not know for certain how it compares to blown malt in terms of flavor and color, but we can assume there is some continuity in production methods over the years, and therefore there is a reasonable similarity between the two malts.

So we have to ask the questions—was all the starch degraded in blown malt? If not, then how could it be hydrolyzed in the mash if it contained no enzymes? Even if it

The brewer is long gone, but its signage and the pub itself still survive.

was degraded in the malt, was it actually broken right down to fermentable sugars? If so, could it then be leached with hot water, rather than mashed, just like modern crystal malt? Given the difficulty of controlling conditions in the drying process, then surely the worts produced would have varied a great deal in fermentability by yeast?

Which leads to the most important question of all—*was brown malt really the only grain used in porter brewing?* Taking the above into account, it seems more likely that early to mid-eighteenth century porter was produced from *a **mixture** of pale and brown malts.* We do know that this became normal practice after the 1780s, but there is little direct evidence that this was the case earlier. The only written evidence on this is that in the supplement to the 1750 edition of *The London and Country Brewer*, Ellis offers an improved method for making porter, using a 1:3 mixture of pale and brown malts. But with the doubt that I have cast on his testimony, can we really believe what he says here?

So there are no definitive answers to the questions I asked above, adding yet another layer of mystery to the porter story. But I do intend to continue to try and work out how to make blown malt. If I succeed, then perhaps we shall come closer to at least some of the answers.

Around 1733–35, a Philadelphia brewery owned by a group of partners offered "stout," presumably simply a name for their strongest beer, since it was also their most expensive one. By this time, English coopering techniques had improved so that large wooden vats could now be manufactured, and in 1736, Parsons, a London porter brewer, installed vats of 1,500 UK barrel capacity (2,100 US barrels). In 1741, Truman sold both brown stout and pale stout, these presumably being the brewer's strongest examples of brown and pale beers (see 1765). One year later, Samuel Whitbread started brewing pale and amber ales, and soon after started to produce porter. He opened a new brewery at

Truman offers brown stout
and pale stout
1740

Whitbread opens bigger new brewery
1750

Whitbread commences brewing
1742

Chiswell Street in 1750, by which time he was hiring cellar space in which to mature his porter at over fifty different locations. The expansion of his business was extremely rapid, and he was later to become the largest porter brewer. But at this point, other brewers were already producing porter, notably Truman, Calvert, Parsons, and Thrale. Indeed, Calvert's Hour Glass Brewery was producing over 50,000 UK barrels (about 70,000 US barrels), while Parsons turned out just under 40,000 UK barrels (56,000 US barrels).

By this time, it seems to have been well established that porter was much improved by several months' maturation, which in part led to the idea that it could only be produced in bulk, and its flavor could not be equaled by private or homebrewers. The benefits of maturation were said to be that the beer "became racy and mellow." Did that mean that it developed flavors (such as lactic acid notes) from the micro flora present in the wood? Or does it, as one or two writers suggested, allow a diminution in the "empyreumatic" or burnt flavor coming from the blown malt? Or did that malt give a smoky flavor because of the fuel used to dry it? I am not convinced about the smoky flavor, although it was not unusual for malts at that time to have a smoke character due to drying over wood, fern, or straw.

But the blowing process required drying the malt for a short time over a very intense fire, which may not have imparted much smoke character if properly seasoned wood was used. And the London porter brewers bought in their malt from Hertfordshire (just north of London), where the maltsters are known to have had an ample supply of seasoned hard woods. Actually, one of the main producers of brown malt today is French & Jupp's, still located in this area. So if blown/brown malt did not have a smoky flavor, then the likelihood

Calvert already at 700,000
US barrels of porter
1750

Combrune recommends
use of thermometer
to brewers
1758

First porter brewed outside
London in Sheffield
1758

Guinness starts up
brewing ale
1759

is that maturation changed the flavor through wild yeast or bacterial action. *Brettanomyces* species have been implicated in this, but there is no direct evidence for it, since these species were not isolated until the twentieth century.

A Frenchman operating a brewery in London was the first man to show how the thermometer could be of benefit to the brewer (*Essay on Brewing,* Combrune, 1758). This was the first real step towards an understanding of the science of brewing. He also provided a recipe for porter, but said nothing about the kind of malt used. The first porter produced outside of London was brewed by Thomas Rawson in 1758 in Sheffield, Yorkshire, some 200 miles north of London. Just one year later, Arthur Guinness commenced brewing at St. James's Gate in Dublin, Ireland, at first producing only ale. And one year after that came the publication of Obadiah Poundage's letter to *The London Chronicle,* with the earliest suggestion that porter was first brewed in 1722. In that same year (1760), attempts were made to brew porter in Glasgow, Scotland, but these were apparently unsuccessful until Murdoch, Warroch & Co brought in a London-trained brewer some fifteen years later.

Also in 1760, W. Reddington described a homemade gravimetric instrument for measuring the strength of worts. This was really the first use of a form of hydrometer in brewing, but Reddington did not seem to have taken this idea any further. James Baverstock, a brewer in Alton, Hampshire, in southern England was the first to apply the hydrometer to the brewing process, carrying out work in secret because of his father's disapproval of such frippery. This could have been the next great step in the evolution of brewing science, after Combrune's work on the thermometer, but Baverstock did not publish his work until much later (Baverstock, 1785), causing him to lose the publication race to John Richardson as will be discussed in the following pages.

In 1765, Malone and Andrews, who were likely the first Irish brewers of porter (long before Guinness tried his hand at it), won prizes from the Royal Dublin Society for producing porter of a saleable quality. Around this time, Whitbread was still selling a pale stout at a considerably higher price than porter, and Thrale's Anchor Brewery offered pale stout for the first time (stout being an indicator of strength, not style). This was why, when porter brewers began to adopt the term "stout," they often used the name "brown stout" to distinguish it from the pale variety. Interestingly, according to one historian (Mathias, 2013), Thrale's main stock was of mild beer (or new London porter), with only small amounts of stale beer mentioned.

During the 1770s, James Baverstock tried to interest some of the London porter brewers in his hydrometer work. Samuel Whitbread totally rebuffed his ideas, but Henry Thrale expressed interest and carried out experiments, with Dr. Johnson observing the tests. But little seems to have come of this, and no other brewers considered using a hydrometer until Richardson published his work nearly a decade later.

During this period, English porter brewers still dominated the Irish market, with Barclay and Whitbread together accounting for 80 percent of the porter consumed in Dublin. On the other hand, 1776 saw the first porter brewed in America by Robert Hare in Philadelphia (Baron, 1962). Although Hare usually gets the credit for this, he was actually only a part-owner of the brewery, along with J. Warren. Before that, porter was regularly imported into America from England, so perhaps the fact that it happened in this year was no accident. There seems to be little record of the amounts brought in from England, but they were presumably fairly small. Note that George Washington is said to have been very fond of Hare's porter, whose fame seems to have spread very rapidly, and Hare appears to have had a number of distributors, which was unusual for a domestic brewery at that time.

In 1781, Ralph Thrale died and his brewery was bought by a Quaker consortium and re-named Barclay, Perkins. Dr. Johnson, the famous lexicographer and a longtime friend of the Thrales, is said to

Baverstock uses hydrometer
as a brewing tool
1765

Malone & Andrews brew a
prize-winning Irish porter
1765

Whitbread and Thrale each
offer a pale stout
1765

In Philadelphia Hare brews
first US porter
1776

have remarked at the sale: "Sir, we are not here to sell a parcel of boilers and vats, but the potentiality of growing rich beyond the dreams of avarice." Shortly after, in 1784, Goodwyn's in East Smithfield, London, became the first brewery to install a steam engine; Whitbread soon followed suit, as did many of the major London brewers.

John Richardson, a brewer in the Yorkshire town of Hull, published *Statical Estimates of the Materials for Brewing* (1784), in which he dealt with the measurement of original and finishing gravities of beers. He called his instrument a saccharometer, and showed that London porter was brewed at OG 1.071 (17.3°P) and had a finishing gravity of 1.018 (4.6°P). That would make it more of a stout in modern terms, but strengths of beers and ales were generally much higher then than they are today. Interestingly, this is a pretty good level of attenuation (especially in days when yeast properties were not well understood); I have to suggest here that it is unlikely that such a level of attenuation could have been achieved if brown/blown malt was the only grain used in brewing porter.

Richardson also showed what amount of extract could be obtained from a given grain, and that pale malt gave considerably more extract per unit volume than did brown malt, so that the latter might be more expensive to use, although apparently cheaper to buy. I can't be certain that this was actually true (although I have earlier written that it was so), because the limited evidence available from the time shows that porter malt was not necessarily significantly cheaper than pale malt on a per quarter basis. The eminent English beer historian Peter Mathias (1959) listed the prices of Hertfordshire pale and brown from 1741 to 1830, and this showed that brown was often 10 to 15 percent cheaper per quarter than pale. However, prices were very variable, and in some

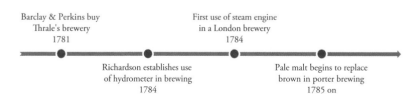

Barclay & Perkins buy
Thrale's brewery
1781

First use of steam engine
in a London brewery
1784

Richardson establishes use
of hydrometer in brewing
1784

Pale malt begins to replace
brown in porter brewing
1785 on

years there was little difference between the cost of the two malts, while in a few years, brown malt was actually more expensive than pale! Note also that Richardson gave extracts on the basis of "pounds/quarter," and since the quarter was a volume and not a weight measure and brown/blown malt was less dense than pale malt, the former had to give a lower extract than the latter on a *volume* basis, for what that is worth.

Now with the two instruments, the thermometer and the hydrometer, brewing science had a firm foundation. But Richardson measured gravities on the basis of "brewer's pounds per barrel," which meant the excess weight of a 36 UK gallon barrel of beer over the weight of a barrel of water, and remained in common use well into the twentieth century, before being replaced by the much more sensible specific gravity.

In response to Richardson, James Baverstock published *Hydrometrical Observations and Experiments in the Brewery* (1785). Sadly, he proposed using specific gravity, but Richardson got there first, and history is written by the victors! In fact, if Richardson hadn't gotten there first, there may have been no need for Balling and his successor Plato to have developed their scale, based on percent sucrose.

Whitbread reached an annual production rate of 150,000 UK barrels (210,000 US barrels) of porter in 1787. The major rivals were John Calvert with 131,000 UK barrels (184,000 US barrels), Barclay Perkins at 106,000 UK barrels (150,000 US barrels), and Truman at 95,000 UK barrels (130,000 US barrels). In this year, the total produced by the major London porter brewers amounted to almost 1,200,000 UK barrels (1,700,000 US barrels). No other brewing center in the world could come close to this, and the scale of American brewing was still tiny and insignificant by comparison.

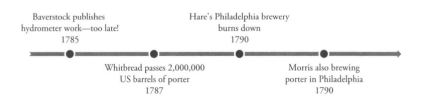

Baverstock publishes
hydrometer work—too late!
1785

Hare's Philadelphia brewery
burns down
1790

Whitbread passes 2,000,000
US barrels of porter
1787

Morris also brewing
porter in Philadelphia
1790

Robert Hare's Philadelphia brewery had already experienced some difficulties and were unable to brew from 1777 to 1778 because of the British occupation of Philadelphia. Worse was to come in 1790, when the brewery burned down, much to George Washington's disgust. He ordered porter from Richard Morris's Dock and Pearl Street Brewery in the same city, indicating that porter brewing was already well established there. Interestingly, the first Morris's Brewery was established over a hundred years earlier, having been founded in 1687. But the Dock and Pearl Street brewery was founded by Morris's grandson in 1745, and it was his grandson who brewed the beer for Washington. It seems likely that some American porters were brewed from ingredients other than those used by English brewers, such as treacle, molasses, and maple syrup, along with herbs and spices. The use of these substitutes probably simply reflected the high cost and lack of availability of English brown malt and hops at that time; I have not seen any evidence that brown malt was being produced in America during that period.

THE RACKING CELLAR.

Racking cellar at Taylor's Albany Brewery 1866.

The building of ever-larger coopered wooden storage vats had been a running competition between London brewers ever since the 1730s, but was coming towards its end in 1790 when Meux built a vat large enough for 200 people to dine in on its completion. Meux followed this up by erecting an even bigger one in 1795, which held 20,000 UK barrels (about 28,000 US barrels) of porter; that would be a quite respectable *annual* output for a modern US craft brewery. In 1814, one of Meux's vats burst, and the escaping porter did considerable damage to surrounding buildings and killed eight people. But the vats lived on, in some cases to modern times. Indeed, some wooden vats from George's Bristol Brewery are still in service for storing (hard) cider at Westons Cider Mill in Herefordshire, England.

In the 1790s, English brewers began to use substitutes for brown malt, which would supposedly give the characteristic porter flavor at a much lower cost than previously. Many writers (including myself at some point) ascribed this to the hydrometer having shown the relatively low extract obtained from a quarter of brown/blown malt, but it may well have been partly because of increasing prices for all malts and increasing taxes as England prepared for the coming wars with Napoleon's France. These "substitutes" included things like ferrous sulfate, alum, and salt to give the porter a good frothy head, as well as capsicum, ginger, quassia, coriander, and more poisonous substances such as *Cocculus indicus,* opium, *Strychnos nux-vomica* (a source of strychnine), and sulfuric acid. These were generally used by unscrupulous publicans, since they could give a young and cheaper beer the same flavor as aged porter. The major London porter brewers such as Truman, Whitbread, and Barclay, Perkins strenuously denied using such materials, and there is no actual evidence to suggest they did. Nevertheless, it

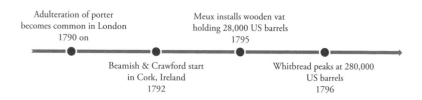

Adulteration of porter
becomes common in London
1790 on

Meux installs wooden vat
holding 28,000 US barrels
1795

Beamish & Crawford start
in Cork, Ireland
1792

Whitbread peaks at 280,000
US barrels
1796

seems clear that such adulterations were the first step in the decline in popularity of porter among English drinkers.

Beamish & Crawford founded the Cork porter brewery in Cork, Ireland, in 1792. Having been ahead of Guinness in porter brewing, Beamish & Crawford soon became the leading Irish brewers in production terms. They maintained that position until 1833, when Guinness overtook them and never looked back. The Beamish & Crawford brewery survived into the twenty-first century, although it changed hands several times. Its stout brand is still extant, but brewed under the Heineken umbrella.

Whitbread became the first brewer to churn out 200,000 UK barrels (280,500 US barrels) of porter in 1796. Its closest rival, Barclay, Perkins was only producing 138,000 UK barrels (194,000 US barrels). But this was to be Whitbread's peak, and it went into something of a decline, with production falling to almost 100,000 UK barrels (140,000 US barrels) in the early part of the nineteenth century, and not climbing back to the 200,000 barrel mark until 1823, by which time Barclay, Perkins surpassed them with 350,000 UK barrels (490,000 US barrels). In 1796, a 4,000 US barrel brewery was erected in Albany, New York; this was to later become the Albany Brewing Company. It brewed nothing but ale and porter until 1896, when a lager brewing department was added.

Joseph Bramah, the noted inventor of the hydraulic press, invented the first beer engine in 1797. The aim of this ingenious device was not just to serve the beer at the bar, but to permit the mixing of "mild" and "stale" porter. In this case, "mild" meant new or fresh and referred to beer that had not been stored in vats, whereas "stale" meant the opposite. This brings in an interesting point, for it suggests that publicans

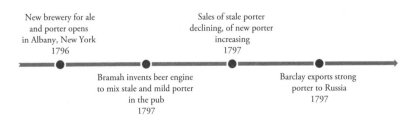

New brewery for ale
and porter opens
in Albany, New York
1796

Bramah invents beer engine
to mix stale and mild porter
in the pub
1797

Sales of stale porter
declining, of new porter
increasing
1797

Barclay exports strong
porter to Russia
1797

had been mixing mild and stale themselves for some time. It raises the question as to whether even the brewers themselves had blended mild and stale before shipping the casks to the brewery. There doesn't appear to be any concrete evidence of this in the early stages of porter brewing. Indeed, Truman was selling both "Intire Mild" and "Intire Stale" in 1743. If brewers were mixing mild and stale themselves, it would answer the always nagging question as to why the porter brewers grew so rapidly when they had to tie up so much capital in storing the beer. In fact, what we are seeing in 1797 is a trend away from stale and towards mild beers (and later to pale beers) by drinkers, a trend which was to accelerate into the nineteenth century. And indeed, we know brewers were mixing mild and stale at the brewery by then.

Barclay, Perkins started to export porter to Russia in this year, supposedly to Catherine the Great herself. It has been suggested that Russian interest in English beer came from Peter the Great, who had come to like it when living in England, where he studied shipbuilding. But that was in 1697, and he was back in Russia in 1698, where he died in 1725. Therefore, he was unlikely to have had any contact with London porter, although according to the Whitbread archivist, Nicholas Redman, Samuel Whitbread had visited St. Petersburg in 1784 and had probably been presented at the court of Catherine the Great. But there was already considerable trade with Russia in those times, for Burton brewers were selling Burton ales into the Baltic countries. It is not clear whether other porter brewers were exporting to this area, yet it would be surprising if they were not, since one London brewer was already shipping pale ale to India at that time! And in the decade from 1780 to 1790, some of the shipments to Russia by the Burton brewer Benjamin Wilson were carried out of Hull (a port in Yorkshire) on a vessel called the *Porter*.

Of course, the importance of Barclay's porter being sent to Russia was that it was their strongest version of porter, and would have been called some form of stout by other brewers. It became known as Russian Imperial Stout, and was brewed with only relatively small changes to the recipe right up until the 1990s—although by that time it was brewed by Courage, then another Southwark brewer. Barclay's brewery was razed by Courage, who themselves merged with Scottish and Newcastle before being swallowed and torn apart by Heineken and Carlsberg. Imperial stout does not form a part of these brewers' portfolios.

PORTER AND STOUT IN THE NINETEENTH CENTURY

Arthur Guinness brewed only porter from 1799, and in 1801 he produced the first version of West India Porter, the forerunner of Foreign Extra Stout and the beginning of a regular export business to the Caribbean. I have not seen any records to suggest that the London porter brewers were exporting to this area, which is surprising considering their efforts to export elsewhere. Did they just think the market was too small, or that the climate was not suitable for a strong dark beer? Guinness brewed Town Porter, Country Porter, Superior (later to become Extra Stout), Keeping Beer, and West India Porter. The lesser porters were known as "single stout" and the Superior as "double stout." Keeping beer was brewed when the malt quality was good, and could be kept for two to three years before blending with beers made from inferior malt. So the blending of old and young beers was now firmly established in Dublin.

In contrast, Whitbread at this time brewed only two sorts of porter—one from pale, brown, and amber malts, the other from pale and brown only. The former was brewed at OG 1.054 (13.3°P), and the latter at 1.050 (12.4°P), both of them significantly lower in gravity than those tested by Richardson some twenty years earlier. This highlights an important point about using the saccharometer—not only did it tell the brewer how strong his beer was, but it also allowed him to decide how strong he wanted it to be! We take that for granted now, but in

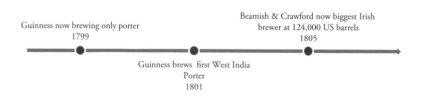

Guinness now brewing only porter
1799

Beamish & Crawford now biggest Irish brewer at 124,000 US barrels
1805

Guinness brews first West India Porter
1801

those days, this was a huge step forward in brewing technology. Barclay, Perkins brewed both a pale and a brown stout, indicating that the term "stout" was not yet limited to dark beers. Beamish & Crawford were now the largest brewer in Ireland, at 100,000 UK barrels (124,000 US barrels), which put it only just below the biggest London brewers.

Up until 1815, England and her European allies had been involved in the so-called Napoleonic Wars. Needless to say, beer prices came under pressure as taxation intensified to pay for the war, and the use of malt substitutes became more prevalent, with some efforts made to find something less likely to kill the drinker. Note above that Whitbread was still using a proportion of brown malt, as were probably most of the major porter brewers. Matthew Wood patented a form of malt extract for the coloring and flavoring of porter in 1802. He wasn't the first to make such an extract, for in 1772, a certain Humphrey Jackson had produced a sufficient amount of concentrated malt extract to go with Captain James Cook on his second voyage, as well as on his third and last. But Jackson's extract was intended to prevent scurvy among sailors on very long voyages. A somewhat related product also became popular as a porter coloring agent, since reduction in the amount of brown malt meant a loss in color as well as of flavor. This was essentia bina, a form of highly burnt sugar, having been set on fire after the initial caramelization (see the Recipe chapter for more details). Obviously this was an extreme form of caramel, and caramel flavors and colorings were used for many years to convert pale beers into dark ones; there is even a porter coloring caramel product still produced today in the United States.

A brewery was founded in 1805 in Newark, New Jersey, which was leased to Peter Ballantine in 1840. He brewed ale and porter there and

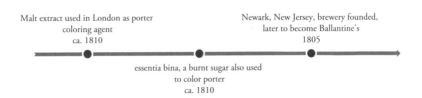

Malt extract used in London as porter
coloring agent
ca. 1810

Newark, New Jersey, brewery founded,
later to become Ballantine's
1805

essentia bina, a burnt sugar also used
to color porter
ca. 1810

added a lager brewery in 1879. Ballantine and Co. survived through Prohibition and was still brewing porter and brown stout in 1939. Ballantine was brewing an India Pale Ale when I came to this country in 1978, and I remember it fondly, as it was one of the very few good American beers available then. For the record, having gone through a multiplicity of ownerships, the Ballantine name now belongs to Pabst, and Ballantine Ale is still available and is contract-brewed for Pabst at Miller's brewery in Eden, North Carolina. In 1810, American breweries were still fairly small in comparison to those in England, since at this time there were 129 of them producing a total of 185,000 US barrels. That's an average of fewer than 1,500 barrels per brewery; we do more than half that today at BrüRm@BAR, our small brewpub in New Haven! Around this time, Embree's brewery was producing ale and porter in Cincinnati, but apparently went out of business by 1836.

Matthew Vassar opened what we would now call a brewpub for a year in 1812 before building a more substantial brewery. He was selling Poughkeepsie Porter, Philadelphia Porter, and London Brown Stout. Stanley Baron, the US brewery historian (1962), suggests that only Poughkeepsie Porter was brewed by Vassar himself. His brewery produced just slightly fewer than 15,000 US barrels by 1841, and is reported to have reached 30,000 US barrels by 1860, some of which was exported to the Caribbean. But the brewery went into a decline and was sold by the nephew of Matthew Vassar in 1899. Baron attributes the decline of the brewery to Vassar's insistence on brewing ales and porter in the face of the growing success of lager brewing.

British troops burned the contents of the Congressional Library in 1814, and Thomas Jefferson offered books from his own collection

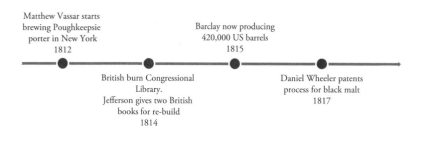

Matthew Vassar starts
brewing Poughkeepsie
porter in New York
1812

British burn Congressional
Library.
Jefferson gives two British
books for re-build
1814

Barclay now producing
420,000 US barrels
1815

Daniel Wheeler patents
process for black malt
1817

to restart it. Among these were two English books—*The London and Country Brewer*, and Michael Combrune's *Theory and Practice of Brewing*. No wonder Brits and Americans have a special relationship! One year later, Barclays had overtaken Whitbread and produced 300,000 UK barrels (420,000 US barrels) of beer.

In 1817, Daniel Wheeler patented the use of a drum-roaster for producing what we would now call black malt, though it was then called "patent malt," an appellation that is still sometimes used today. This was a turning point in porter and stout brewing, for it was now no longer necessary to use porter colorings and malt substitutes. Instead, it was possible to add a small proportion of black malt and to reduce, or even eliminate, the use of brown/blown malt, with pale malt still being the main workhorse, of course. Perhaps the most important result of this invention was that it set the stage for the development of stout as a truly separate style of its own, rather than simply being a stronger form of porter.

Brewers certainly took up the use of black malt, although with varying rates of alacrity. Guinness were one of the quickest to do so, using it in 1817, at first along with some brown malt, but replacing it completely by 1828 and using a grist containing 4 to 5.5 percent black malt, and the rest pale malt. Whitbread had tested black malt in 1817, but still kept up the use of brown malt; Barclay was using black malt by 1820. In the same year black malt was patented, Guinness shipped eight hogsheads (16 US barrels) of porter to a John Heavy in South Carolina. It is not clear if this was their first shipment to America, since they had already been shipping porter to the West Indies for some time. Other changes were noticeable too, for by this time, 90 percent

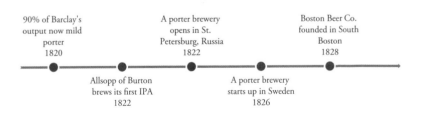

90% of Barclay's output now mild porter 1820

Allsopp of Burton brews its first IPA 1822

A porter brewery opens in St. Petersburg, Russia 1822

A porter brewery starts up in Sweden 1826

Boston Beer Co. founded in South Boston 1828

of Barclay's production was "mild" porter, marking a huge change in drinking tastes.

In the early 1820s, Russian protective tariffs were introduced at such a high rate that the Russian market for British brewers collapsed. It is not clear as to what that did immediately to Barclay's Brown Stout, which had been developed for export to Russia, but we do know it was still being brewed by the 1830s. We also know that a porter brewery was set up in St. Petersburg in 1822 by a Mr. Stein, who had once sat as an English M.P., in order to feed the continuing Russian demand for such beer. A porter brewery was established in Sweden in 1826, closing that market to English brewers. 1822 was a very important year in another way, in that this was when the Burton brewer Samuel Allsopp decided to venture into the Indian market for pale ale. Soon the drinking public were going to prefer not just mild porter over the vatted version—they were going to prefer pale to dark beers.

In this period, Guinness's Town Porter (or single stout) was brewed at OG 1.064 (15.7°P), while Extra Superior Porter (double stout) came in at 1.082 (19.8°P). West India Porter was brewed to the same OG as the latter, but was more highly hopped to make it suitable for export to the Caribbean. An 1820 brewing treatise gives a detailed description of a method of brewing London brown stout porter.

Meanwhile, in 1821 came the founding of what would become Bunker Hill Breweries (and later A. G. Van Nostrand) in Charlestown, Massachusetts. Attempts to revive it after Prohibition, first as Bunker Hill Breweries, then as Van Nostrand Brewing Co., were unsuccessful. Prior to Prohibition, the brewery produced Old Stout, Porter, and the unpleasant-sounding Old Musty Ale. Seven years after this was when

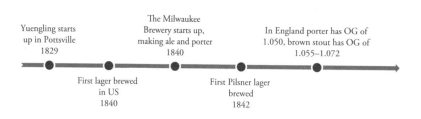

Yuengling starts
up in Pottsville
1829

The Milwaukee
Brewery starts up,
making ale and porter
1840

In England porter has OG of
1.050, brown stout has OG of
1.055–1.072

First lager brewed
in US
1840

First Pilsner lager
brewed
1842

the Boston Beer Company was incorporated in South Boston, Massachusetts, presumably brewing ale and porter. It apparently continued brewing until Prohibition, then restarted in 1936, but closed in 1956 under the name of Imperial Brewing Co. The name Boston Beer Company was adopted by Jim Koch in 1984, and this new company has since become one of the most successful and largest brewing companies of the new wave in America.

D. C. Yuengling, an emigrant from Germany, built a brewery in Pottsville, Pennsylvania, in 1829. It burned down in 1831, but was rebuilt at what is now the current site of Yuengling's main brewery. It is not clear when Yuengling started brewing his porter, but it was likely to have been around this time, because porter brewing was already well established in Pennsylvania. It was a little too early for this to have been bottom-fermented, despite Yuengling's origin, as lager brewing did not gain a foothold in America until 1840. I am not sure when lager was introduced by Yuengling, but they were certainly brewing it in 1873.

William Haas and Andrew Sulzer started a brewery in 1833, which by 1841 became known as Lill & Diversey. This was stated to be the largest brewery in the West, and it continued to brew ale and porter up until 1871, when it was destroyed in the Great Chicago Fire. In England, the trend away from porter and stout was emphasized by Whitbread, as they ceased to brew only these beers and commenced ale production. Barclay, Perkins and other porter brewers had begun to brew ale in the previous year. In

A later ad for Yuengling's Porter—he looks happy!

1836, the twelve major London brewers produced a total of 2,200,000 UK barrels (almost 3,100,000 US barrels).

John Wagner, a Bavarian immigrant in Philadelphia, commenced lager brewing in 1840, having brought "bottom-fermenting" yeast with him from Germany. He produced only on a small scale, and the first "large-scale" lager brewery is reckoned to have been established by Charles Engel and Charles Wolf in 1844. The first pilsner lager was brewed just before that, in 1842 by Josef Groll, and the worldwide trend towards drinking pale beers was truly under way. The Milwaukee Brewery, the first in Milwaukee, began brewing ale and porter in 1840. It continued to produce these beers, later under the name M.W. Powell & Co., until it closed in 1880, being unable to compete with the lager brewers of that city.

At this point, 53 percent of Guinness's total production was exported to Scotland and England. Some 82 percent of that production was of Extra Superior Porter, which became known as Double Stout, and later as Extra Stout. In the 1840s, the rise in popularity of pale beers in England took a firm hold, for this was a decade of major expansion in the railway system there. Burton-on-Trent's brewers could now transport their pale ales all over the country relatively cheaply and rapidly, putting pressure on the country brewers—as well as those in London—to start producing pale ales themselves. In 1843, one author records common porter having OG 1.050 (12.4°P) and brown stout as falling in the range of 1.055 to 1.072 (13.6°P to 17.5°P).

Stout as a style evolved over a fairly long period. But by 1850, the use of the term "stout" as denoting a beer in its own right had become widely accepted. Just six years earlier, Whitbread produced no fewer than four stouts of differing strengths. Barclay, Perkins had Imperial Brown Stout at 1.107 (26.5°P), as well as Export Brown Stout at 1.093 (22.3°P). Other brewers simply listed single and double stouts, both always more expensive than regular porter. In the 1850s in America, the conversion to pale lager drinking was still in its early stages, as the really big influx of European immigrants was yet to come. At this time, there were 431 breweries producing a total of 750,000 US barrels of beer (compare that to the 1836 total of 3.1 million US barrels produced by just twelve London brewers). No less than 81 percent of this was brewed in New York and Pennsylvania, and much of that would have been ale, porter, and stout. It seems that some of the German brewers who had already arrived saw porter as so popular that they had to make their own versions of this beer, fermented with lager yeast. Indeed, there is some evidence that Philadelphia porter was being exported to the Caribbean, South America, and even India at this time. In a reversal of the trend towards lager, Charles Bierbauer (doesn't that translate as "Beer Builder"?) started a lager brewery in 1853 in Utica, New York, and ale and porter were added to the company's products later.

Also in 1856, the London brewer Ind Coope opened a brewery in Burton to produce their own India Pale Ale; others would soon follow. Murphy's Ladywell brewery was established in Cork, Ireland, principally as a brewer of stout. It never quite managed to match Guinness, although in 1906 its production was second only to that of Guinness. Murphy did produce porter as well as stout, but porter brewing effectively ceased in 1943. Today, Murphy's Stout still competes with Beamish & Crawford and Guinness, although Murphy's and Beamish are both now owned by Heineken, and Beamish's Stout is actually produced at what was once Murphy's brewery!

By 1856, brewing had spread to the West Coast of the United States; lager brewers generally dominated, but in this year there were two ale and porter brewers operating in San Francisco: the Eagle Brewery and the Eureka Brewery. The porter from Eureka Brewery won first prize and a diploma in a San Francisco Industrial Exhibition held in 1857. Also in 1856, production of pale ale, porter, and brown stout in Philadelphia amounted to 170,000 US barrels—still less than that of any of the great London brewers. This represented 48 percent of the city's production, but ominously (for our story), the other 52 percent was made up by lager beer.

Earlier, in 1849, Guinness had started to brew Triple Stout to supply the export trade of E. & J. Burke, Dublin bottlers. This beer was also described as Foreign Export Double Stout, later shortened to Foreign Extra Stout, or FES. In 1860, total Guinness production amounted to 140,000 Irish barrels (a shade under 175,000 US barrels).

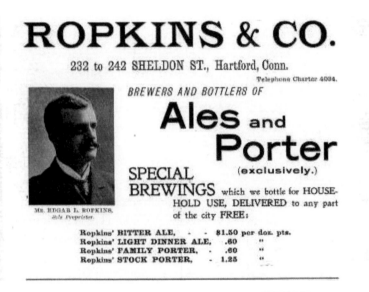

Two pre-Prohibition ads for Connecticut brewed Porter, both featuring "Stock Porter."

Guinness brews Triple Stout
for export
1849

Ind Coope first London
brewer to start Burton brewery
1856

Murphy's of Cork start
as stout brewers
1856

E. & J. Burke had started exporting to America, and later to Australia and South Africa; in 1860, Burke sold some 4,000 hogsheads (8,000 US barrels). However, Guinness hadn't established itself in America at this time, and would even have problems doing so into the twentieth century. The English market was always its biggest target after Ireland. In 1864, Guinness brewed 53 percent of the total Dublin output of beer, and had a 45.5 percent share of the Irish trade to England.

An organization of brewers was founded in 1864 that was to become the United States Brewers' Association. It was a measure of the rise of lager brewing that, until 1875, German (not English) was the official Convention language, and transactions were published in both German and English. Because of this, few, if any, ale brewers joined the organization.

It was supposedly also in 1864 when the Washington Brewery was established as the first in Seattle and brewed porter, lager, and cream ale. In this year, Whitbread in London was still turning out more porter and stout than ale. Their range was quite wide and included porter at OG 1.053 (13.1°P), contract porter at 1.060 (14.7°P), keeping porter at 1.058 (14.3°P), single stout at 1.085 (20.4°P), keeping single stout at 1.081 (19.6°P), and export stout at 1.071 (17.3°P). How curious that the keeping and export stouts should have a lower OG than the regular single stout!

About 1869, Belgian entrepreneur A. LeCoq had established a trade exporting beer from England to Russia and the Baltic. The story goes that he gave generous amounts of beer to wounded Russian soldiers during the Crimean War. Accordingly, the tsar awarded him an imperial warrant, so that the Barclay's stout he was shipping could now be called "Imperial Russian Stout."

The decade of the 1870s was a momentous period in the brewing industry, with pale beers becoming dominant in both England and

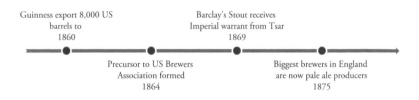

Guinness export 8,000 US
barrels to
1860

Barclay's Stout receives
Imperial warrant from Tsar
1869

Precursor to US Brewers
Association formed
1864

Biggest brewers in England
are now pale ale producers
1875

America. First, several London brewers opened breweries in Burton itself during this decade, so they could produce IPA to match the Burton brewers. Notable among these was the great porter brewer, Truman's. And in 1875, Whitbread, for the first time, brewed more ale than porter or stout. More importantly, Bass brewed almost 1,000,000 UK barrels (1,400,000 US barrels), most of it pale ale, closely followed by another Burton enterprise, Allsopp, at 900,000 UK barrels (almost 1,300,000 US barrels). The London brewers were led by Truman's 600,000 UK barrels (close to 850,000 US barrels). And they were threatened from another direction, for Guinness had now reached a similar production level with 400,000 hogsheads (about 800,000 US barrels). Guinness was pushing English brewers out of the stout market in their own country, and would continue to do so until there was virtually no home production of porter and stout at all. But that would not be the case until well into the next century. However, Guinness didn't have everything their own way, as we can see from an 1877 price list from a London bottler who offered the following:

From Burton: Bass Extra Stout and Imperial Stout (they weren't just IPA brewers!)

From Scotland: Archibald Arrol's XXX Stout, McEwan's Extra Stout, and Tennant's XXX Stout

From London: Barclay, Perkins's Extra Double Stout and Imperial Double Stout

The most surprising thing is the presence of the Bass Imperial Stout. Barclay's must have had a fairly good trade in their Imperial Double Stout if Bass considered it worth their while to compete with it.

At the beginning of this decade, Guinness had adopted refrigeration, with machines using ether as a refrigerant. But more important was the invention by Linde in 1876 of the ammonia absorption refrigerator, which was to revolutionize brewing, not only by permitting better control of the process, but also to enable transportation over long distances without spoilage problems. This was to be most important in America, where Anheuser-Busch was the first to ship beer in refrigerated rail cars in 1877. Refrigeration really meant the end of breweries dominating in their own localities; competition could now come in from almost anywhere in the country. Further advances were apparent in this decade; with the wider availability of glass, bottling on a large, mechanized scale was now possible. And the technology of pasteurizing beer was developing rapidly, reducing the risk of spoilage of the beer in bottling. All these advances favored the shipping brewer over his local counterpart. This, coupled with the population growth in the United States, ensured that the larger breweries had joined the Industrial Revolution and some of them would grow much bigger still, as the British brewers had already done. Indeed, it raised the idea that there could come a time when three major brewing companies might have locked in more than 80 percent of the American brewing business! A footnote to this was that Adolph Coors advertised in a Denver, Colorado, directory in 1873 that he was a dealer in "bottled beer, ale, porter, and cider" a year or so before the opening of his Golden Brewery.

By 1880, growth in American brewing was shown by the fact that production from 2,830 breweries totaled 9,473,000 US barrels, with New York producing 34 percent of the total. Note that there seems to be some doubt about this total, as a second source puts it at 12,800,900! An American publication of that year lists English brown stout at 8.5% abv and London porter at 6.0% abv (both numbers seem to be a little high), but offers no such numbers for American versions of these beers. Just two years later, brewing in the United States had expanded greatly to a total national output of 14,000,000 US barrels. As immigration to the United States continued to increase, so did the beer output, which continued to climb for the next forty years. How much of this production was of porter and/or stout is unknown, but it is fact that in 1882, Guinness output of stout and porter reached 1,000,000 Irish Barrels (about 1,240,000 US barrels), making it the biggest brewer in the UK sphere. The decade of the 1890s saw another important advance in bottling procedures, with William Painter's invention in 1892 of the crown cap, a device far superior to the corks and porcelain swing stoppers used previously.

By this time, lager beer dominated the American brewing scene, especially in the Midwest, although porter and stout still retained some popularity in the Northeast. Indeed, it was not yet out of the picture even in the lager "heartlands," for some time after the 1870s, Coors had apparently brewed a porter aged for eight months. And in 1899, Anheuser-Busch brewed an American porter, sold as "Black & Tan." That is interesting, since I was under the impression that a Black and Tan was actually a mixture of stout and bitter ale, poured carefully so that the two layers remained distinct. I had been led to believe that the juxtaposition of Irish stout over British ale had been devised in Ireland to shake a fist at the British, and in particular at the notorious soldiers sent from Britain to police Ireland during the First World War, who were known as "Black and Tans" because of their distinctive uniforms.

Also during this period, Yuengling was advertising Wiener beer, porter, ale, and even a brown stout. I have been unable to discover when they commenced, or even ceased, brewing stout. Exports and imports of malt (mainly to and from Britain and Germany) were very small at less than 1 percent of total US malt production in the decades from 1880 to 1901. It therefore seems doubtful that any significant amount of English brown malt was imported into the United States at this time. Meanwhile, back across the water, Maclay of Alloa in Scotland brewed Original Oatmeal Stout in 1895. This appears to have been the first oatmeal stout as such, although the use of oats as a brewing grain had been common centuries earlier. Oatmeal stout became relatively popular quite quickly, which was probably partly due to a health craze at the time, further exemplified by the introduction of "milk stout" some ten years or so later. A large number of British brewers hopped on the oatmeal stout bandwagon, and both Barclay, Perkins and Whitbread brewed versions of it in the 1920s and 1930s. However, these two brewers used only 0.5 percent of oats in the grain bill for these beers, an amount too little to have any effect on flavor (or

Painter invents the crown cap
1890s

Maclay of Scotland brews first Oatmeal Stout
1895

Yuengling offers Brown Stout and porter
1890s

Anheuser-Busch makes an American porter (Black & Tan)
1899

health, for that matter), suggesting that this was nothing more than a cynical marketing exercise!

PORTER AND STOUT IN THE TWENTIETH CENTURY

Although lager brewing was now firmly entrenched in America, porter was still widely available. West of the Mississippi, it was being produced by at least twenty brewing companies, notably by the Seattle Ale & Porter Co. and the Robert Witz Brewery in Sitka, Alaska, as well as Lebanon Valley Brewing in Lebanon, Pennsylvania, and Oneida Brewing Co. from Utica, New York. It still held a strong position in Philadelphia, being offered by John F. Betz & Son, the successors to Robert Hare's brewery, as well as Begner & Engel and American Brewing. The John Roehm Brewery actually provided an "Imitation English Porter," the exact nature of which was not clear. Was it a "true imitation" with brown malt, or did it simply indicate American porters were different from their English counterparts? Did it even suggest that American porter brewers were simply adding caramel coloring to pale beers, or that they were still using yet other ingredients, such as molasses?

Porter was no stranger to New England drinkers and a notable example was Narragansett Porter which was still brewed in Rhode Island in the 1970s. New Hampshire had several brewers of our "brown beauty," such as Mountain Spring Brewery out of Walpole, which offered a brown stout porter around the turn of the century. True W. Jones Brewing Co. in Manchester, New Hampshire, produced porter up until Prohibition, and the Portsmouth Brewing Co.

Porter still widely brewed in Northeast US
1900s

Mountain Spring, Walpole,
Massachusetts, sells Brown Stout
Porter
1900s

Hull's Brewery, New Haven,
Connecticut, offers Stock Porter
1916

had an Old Brown Stout before it died a similar death. True W. Jones had learned the brewmaster trade in the Bay State Brewery in Boston, which was owned by his brother, Frank Jones. The latter operated the biggest brewery in New Hampshire, which also offered porter and brown stout up until Prohibition.

I must also make some mention of Connecticut, and of New Haven in particular. It is true that the biggest concern at the end of the nineteenth century was Fresenius & Sons, with 100,000 barrels of lager beer. However, most other companies produced a mix of lager, ale, and porter, such as the Yale Brewing Company, which resurfaced as the New Haven Brewing Company after Prohibition. Another notable concern was Hull's Brewing Co., which in 1916 was offering not only ale and porter, but also Stock Ale and Stock Porter, only the second American reference I have seen to long-matured porter. Hull's was still brewing ales in the 1950s, and finally closed in 1977. No brewery operated in the city for a brief period, until Elm City Brewing Co. opened in 1989, only to close in 1998. But BrüRm@BAR opened in 1996 and is still flourishing; the brewer Jeff Browning unashamedly calls himself "a brewer of English ales." A stout is one of BAR's staples, and Jeff also brews various specialty porters, many of them based on my historical research. So the thread of ale brewing has been virtually continuous in New Haven ever since beer was first produced there!

Guinness, not satisfied with dominating the British stout market, was still targeting the American drinker. In 1884, E. & J. Burke sold some 50,000 hogsheads (100,000 US barrels) of Guinness Foreign Extra Stout, but these imports had gradually decreased up until 1900. It has been suggested that this was because American drinkers saw it

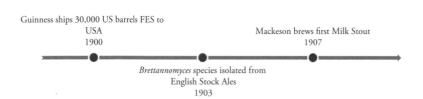

Guinness ships 30,000 US barrels FES to USA
1900

Mackeson brews first Milk Stout
1907

Brettannomyces species isolated from English Stock Ales
1903

chiefly as a tonic, but Burke and Guinness made some extra efforts in the early part of this century. They increased sales of FES in the United States from 15,000 hogsheads (30,000 US barrels) in 1900 to 38,000 hogsheads (76,000 US barrels) in 1914, the latter representing no less than 70 percent of total American beer imports. In 1910, Burke had stopped bottling for the American market in Liverpool, England, and instead commenced bottling FES in New York. By 1915, there were no fewer than seven authorized FES bottlers in New York. But, of course, all this business was to collapse under the twin onslaughts of World War I and of Prohibition.

This decade also saw the arrival on the English scene of milk stout, brewed in 1907 by Mackeson in Kent, England. It of course got its name because it was brewed with a portion of milk sugar (lactose), which is not fermented by yeast. We are back on the health kick here— we saw above that Guinness was regarded as a tonic in the United States, and in general, stout was held to be a nourishing drink. Guinness was to make much of this later on, with their succession of adverts based on the phrase "Guinness is Good for You." So what could be healthier still than a beer based on milk, which we all know is good for us? There is no magic in stout, and it is no more nourishing than any other beer, whether or not it contains milk sugar. And the British government banned any reference to the word "milk" on beer labels in 1942. Yet milk (now known as sweet) stout did achieve a certain popularity and yielded sales significant enough that the brewery was taken over by Whitbread in 1929. By 1960, Mackeson sales, at over 400,000 UK barrels (560,000 US barrels), accounted for more than half Whitbread's home trade. It is still produced today, though now under the A-B Inbev umbrella. It is also still produced under license by the Carib Brewery in Trinidad, and it seems to have been produced here in the United States by the Boston Brewing Company. Other brewers produced their own versions, noticeably Charrington with their Jubilee Stout, which was still available in the late 1970s when I moved to the United States, but does not seem to be around now.

Early in the century (1903), N. H. Claussen isolated the yeast that caused secondary fermentation in English stock ales and called it

Brettanomyces. It is possible to infer that such a yeast species was present during the vatting of the early porters, and that it was responsible for the definitive taste of porter—and perhaps its intoxicating effect, as one writer has suggested. But extrapolating backwards over two centuries is a risky approach, and we cannot be certain that the peculiar flavor of porter was due to other causes (such as the type of malt or brewing procedures), or to the effect of certain organisms. Indeed, we just cannot be certain exactly what that "peculiar flavor" of the early porters was at all!

In 1905, Privatbrauerei Hoepfner in Karlsruhe, Germany, was said to have brewed a porter. It was supposedly in the English style, but called Deutsch Porter for political reasons. In that same year in the United States, *Wahl-Henius Handy Book* lists analyses of various porters and stouts. Their results show that an American brown stout (not named) came in at OG 1.075 (18.2°P), while various English and Irish stouts mostly came in at about the same OG. Two American porters are listed, one at OG 1.074 (18.0°P), and the other at 1.054 (13.3°P); these are compared with a Canadian porter at 1.058 (14.3°P) and a Swedish porter at a whopping 1.079 (19.1°P). Curiously, no English porters were included in the list. *Wahl-Henius* also stated that for porters and stouts, "it is best to use mixed malts, i.e. a mixture of high and low kiln-dried malts. If these cannot be had, caramel malt, black malt, and sugar coloring to the required amount should be added." Brown malt is mentioned in this quite comprehensive book as being only an English product. Porterine is also mentioned as an additive for beer to make it taste like porter.

Out of the sequence somewhat, but worth including here, are some of the results of a 1917 study by the US Department of Agriculture.

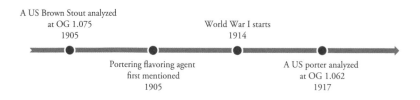

A US Brown Stout analyzed
at OG 1.075
1905

World War I starts
1914

Portering flavoring agent
first mentioned
1905

A US porter analyzed
at OG 1.062
1917

The authors analyzed beers from three unnamed American breweries, which included a brown stout at OG 1.079 (19.1°P), finishing at 1.024 (6.1°P), which would mean it contained 7.2% abv. Lactic acid in the stout was given as 0.56 percent, high enough to give it a sour edge. Four porters were listed, all very similar, with OG 1.062 (15.2°P), and around 5.9% abv, making them somewhat stronger than English porters of the time. Acidity from lactic acid was lower than for the stout, at about 0.3 percent, slightly higher than the 0.27 percent lactic acid Guinness regarded as the limit for their beer to still be saleable! An interesting point about this study is that the porters were quoted as having been brewed from malt, cerealine, and brewer's sugar, with no proportions mentioned. Cerealine appears to have been simply a form of corn flakes, and was therefore an adjunct; whether its use was the rule in porter brewing, or whether it was there as an economy in wartime, is impossible to say. The article did not mention roasted malts, so whether the color (about 60°L) came from that or the sugar is not known. The reason I am going on about this is that there is no direct evidence from these two sources that American brewers used brown malt in their porters and stouts, which is not to say that they did not!

The period from 1914 to 1920 was disastrous for beer because of the "war to end all wars," the idiocy of which is summed up by the fact that both the English king and the German kaiser were grandsons of Queen Victoria! But, no politics, this is about beer, and it was a dreadful time for brewers, especially in this country. Firstly, there were restrictions on brewing supplies in both Britain and the United States, and particularly on the quantity of roasted malts that could be produced. There was no such restriction in Ireland, so it has been suggested by Michael Jackson that this permitted Irish brewers to continue to produce authentic

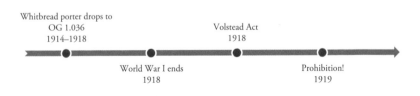

Whitbread porter drops to
OG 1.036
1914–1918

Volstead Act
1918

World War I ends
1918

Prohibition!
1919

porters and stouts, while English brewers, with no option to resort to black and brown malts, could not. I confess that I found that a reasonable explanation at the time, but Ron Pattinson has, I think fairly conclusively, shown that this was not at all the case. Pattinson produced figures from the Whitbread archives that show that the brewer was actually using a *higher* proportion of black and brown malts in their porter and Imperial stout in 1918 than they were in 1914. The decline in porter drinking had nothing to do with the availability of raw materials; it was simply that the drinker now preferred mild, pale, and bitter ales.

The shortage of raw materials did cause a drop in the original gravities of most beers, and porter was no exception. Whitbread's ordinary porter had an OG 1.052 (12.9°P) in 1914, but this had fallen to 1.043 (10.7°P) by 1919, and had been as low as 1.036 (9.0°P) in 1918. Porter strengths were never to recover, as we shall see later. Note that the mild ale, which had been its biggest competitor, was not a derivative of the mild porter I spoke of earlier, as I had once thought, but a quite different beer, brewed somewhat sweeter, without brown malt, and with a relatively low hop rate.

Guinness's porter had fared no better, having been brewed at OG 1.058 (14.3°P) in 1914 and falling to 1.036 (9.0°P) by 1918, while Extra Stout had fallen to 1.050 (12.4°P). When raw materials restrictions were lifted in 1921, ES rose to 1.054 (13.3°P), but porter stayed at 1.036 until 1940, when its OG was raised to 1.041 (10.2°P). From 1918 onwards, Guinness had a problem with increasing acidity in Foreign Extra Stout, due to lower sales resulting in the beer being vatted for a longer time. For the record, towards the end of the nineteenth century, 0.27 percent lactic acid for the beer in vat had been regarded as the saleable limit.

WWI may have had a bad effect on beer quality, but what followed it in the United States—the Volstead Act of 1918, which brought in Prohibition in 1919—did much greater damage to the beer industry in this country. Some breweries managed to continue on by making so-called "near" beer at 0.5% abv, by producing soft drinks, by making malt extract for confectionery products (and for illicit homebrewing!), or whatever else they could do to survive. But many closed up shop entirely, and only a few of these started up again when Prohibition was repealed in 1933 (and many of those breweries are no longer in business today). St. Louis alone had twenty-two breweries before the Act, but only nine brewed again on repeal. In 1916, there were 1,313 breweries in the United States, producing almost 61,000,000 barrels of beer. By 1932, the remaining brewers produced fewer than 3,000,000 barrels of near beer (0.5% abv). After the repeal of Prohibition in 1933, there were 756 breweries, and total output was almost 38,000,000 barrels. A real oddity was that, during Prohibition, Falstaff brewed a "nonalcoholic" Dublin-style stout!

W. C. Fields is reported to have said of Prohibition: "I was forced to live for days on nothing but food and water." But I don't want to dwell on the Ignoble Experiment; it's too depressing a subject. It did not entirely knock out porter brewing in the United States, as might have been expected. As was the case in Britain, porter declined here because of a change in drinking tastes, rather than due to outside effects. But it was still being brewed in the United States after Prohibition, and would continue to be so for another forty years.

Moving on to the thirties: In 1934, E. & J. Burke, the Guinness bottlers, opened a stout and ale brewery on Long Island. In 1943, Guinness bought out Burke, despite the fact that the chairman, Ernest Guinness, favored building a new brewery in Seattle. Five years later, Guinness started to brew Extra Stout at 1.073 (17.7°P), being unable to produce FES because of a lack of maturation vessels. This did not meet with immediate success, and the gravity was gradually decreased to 1.059 (14.5°P), but sales had not reached 30,000 barrels (US, presumably) by 1950, even though the brewery capacity was 75,000 barrels. As a result, the company vacillated about ceasing to brew Burke's

US beer production
61,000,000 barrels
1916

REPEAL!
1933

US beer production
38,000,000 barrels
1934

1,313 breweries in US
1916

736 breweries in US
1934

ale, and spent much more money on advertising both stout and ale than sales could justify. Accordingly, the brewery was closed in 1954. For once, the Guinness marketing magic had deserted them!

The year 1936 saw the first brew in Guinness's new English brewery, at Park Royal North London. Interestingly, it had to be "conditioned" with vat bottoms from Dublin that were introduced to the plant in order to inoculate it with the required mix of bacteria and wild yeast! Not coincidentally, Guinness was still having trouble with acidity in their vatted beers and began to look at ways to control it, coming up with a series of separately aged flavor extracts for FES. These could be added to "young" beers, creating a product that was stable and developed no further acidity. In the meantime, Park Royal went from strength to strength and was producing some 2 million UK barrels (almost 3 million US barrels) by 1956. It remained at this level for some time, but the brewery was closed in 2005, with all stout production returning to Dublin. Park Royal never brewed any porter, and production of it in Dublin had ceased by 1974.

Porter had died a death in England rather earlier. In 1922, at least twelve London brewers still produced porter, and by this time, OGs were in the range of 1.036 to 1.039 (9.0 to 9.8°P), but the writing was well and truly on the wall. In 1937, only six companies were brewing porter in London, and the beer appeared to die completely going into WWII. Whitbread, for example, produced only 3,810 UK barrels (just over 5,000 US barrels) of porter and stout in 1939, which represented only about 3 percent of their total output, according to Ron Pattinson. So it comes as no surprise that they brewed their last batch of porter in 1940. The beer that had underpinned the evolution of large-scale brewers was no longer considered economically viable by them.

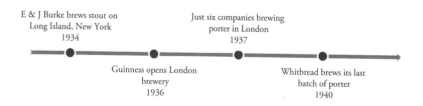

E & J Burke brews stout on
Long Island, New York
1934

Just six companies brewing
porter in London
1937

Guinness opens London
brewery
1936

Whitbread brews its last
batch of porter
1940

In 1937, the Federal Alcohol Administration decreed that beer could not be advertised as ale, stout, or porter unless it contained at least 5 percent alcohol w/w (6.2% abv). I think this ruling later led to the production of malt liquors—strong but bland beers aimed at drinkers who wanted nothing more than to get drunk. And, of course, there were other idiotic rulings, such as those which made homebrewing illegal even after the repeal!

Guinness's heavy presence in Britain did not deter English brewers, and many of them (both large and small) continued to brew their own version of stout, in bottle and on draught. Courage continued intermittent small-scale production of Barclay's Russian Imperial Stout, but there were few other stouts to match it, and it died out before the end of the twentieth century (but has now been revived—see the Definitions chapter). In 1959, Plymouth Breweries offered an Imperial Brown Stout, but this was brewed at only 1.045 (11.2°P). Oatmeal stout appeared to have lost its popularity somewhere around the 1960s, but sweet stouts prevailed in the form of Mackeson and Charrington's Jubilee Stout. But in the 1960s, concentration in the British brewing industry began to intensify, and by the 1970s just six brewing companies held more than 70 percent of the market in Britain—and one of those was Guinness! The long-term trend in favor of pale beers continued, with mild ale sales declining drastically. Bitter ale and today's pale lager came to dominate the market. The latter was to become the most popular style of beer by the late twentieth to early twenty-first centuries.

Consequently, stout became a niche market for most brewers, and most of them ceased to brew it themselves. If they sold any at all, they

Guinness buys out Burke's
Long Island brewery
1943

Guinness closes Long Island
brewery
1954

No porter in England; dry
stout dominated by
Guinness
1950s

Whitbread produces 560,000
US barrels Mackeson Sweet
Stout
1960

would buy it in from one of the big brewers, notably Guinness. If you go into an English pub today and ask for stout, you are most likely to be offered Guinness's, Murphy's, or perhaps Beamish's versions—all, of course, Irish dry stouts! You can obtain stouts produced by English brewers, but these are mostly available in bottle, and this is in any case a recent phenomenon, as we shall see later.

Despite the efforts of WWI, Prohibition, the Great Depression, and WWII, porter brewing did not die out in North America. Right into the 1960s, this beer was still available in the Northeast. Narragansett Brewing offered it in Rhode Island, but Pennsylvania remained the stronghold of porter. It was brewed by Yuengling, Stegmaier, Neuweiler's, Esslinger, Christian Schmidt, and the Fell Brewing Co. in Carbondale, Pennsylvania. However, porter was now only a niche product and clinging to its place in the market, so it is not surprising that only Stegmaier and Yuengling continued to brew it into the 1970s.

In a sense, the modern period from 1970 to 2000 (and on to 2014) is the most important part of the history of porter and stout. Unquestionably, the revival of porter and stout began in this country in the hands of the new craft brewers, although in 2004 Yuengling was reported to be the world's biggest porter brewers (at 80,000 US barrels per annum). Once again, this reverse in the fortunes of porter originated as the result of a change in popular taste, with a revolt against the ubiquitous so-called pilsners that dominated the American market. A section of the drinking public realized that they wanted something better, and a trend towards drinking beers of taste and character began. The first brewer to really see this trend was Fritz Maytag, who had resuscitated the almost-defunct Anchor Brewing Company in San

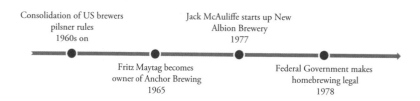

Consolidation of US brewers
pilsner rules
1960s on

Jack McAuliffe starts up New
Albion Brewery
1977

Fritz Maytag becomes
owner of Anchor Brewing
1965

Federal Government makes
homebrewing legal
1978

Francisco, California, in 1965. Maytag brewed Anchor Porter, a real "throwback," in that it was an all-malt beer with OG 1.071 (17.3°P), albeit that it was bottom-fermented. It is a debatable point, but Anchor Brewing is not generally held to have been a microbrewery, so that the honor of setting up the first one in the United States goes to Jack McAuliffe. His New Albion Brewery in Sonoma, California, started its business in 1977, and soon offered not only a porter, but also a stout. The stout was brewed at around 1.053 (13.1°P), with black malt and flaked barley, but no roast barley; unfortunately, I have no details on the porter.

New Albion closed in 1982, but the dam had been broken—doubly so when Bert Grant opened the first brewpub in the United States that year in Yakima, Washington. The craft brewing scene exploded rapidly, with companies like Redhook, Boulder Brewing, Sierra Nevada, and others opening (or already open, in the case of Boulder) and more to come. Bill Owen, with his Buffalo Bill Brewpub, followed very closely on Bert Grant's heels, and a good many more such establishments were

An echo of porter's origins.

to follow. Oh, and by the way, a little outfit called the American Home-brewer's Association (AHA) had come into being just before this in 1978. This was on the heels of a very important piece of legislation in 1978, when the Federal Government legalized homebrewing (the individual states followed this lead, but at very varying rates). With the formation of the AHA, we had what you might call the third piece of the puzzle, in that this organization facilitated the exchange of information on brewing that not only led more people to brew their own, but also helped many of them to found their own breweries and brewpubs. This, in my view, was a very important reason as to why the American craft brewers very soon outstripped those in Britain, the renaissance there having begun about the same time as in the United States.

PORTER AND STOUT IN THE TWENTY-FIRST CENTURY

I could write a lot more about the rise of microbrewing in the United States, but that would be a book on its own. Many of the "early" craft brewers here had a porter or stout in their portfolio, setting a trend that followed right up to the present. As the craft flourished and brewers became more knowledgeable, so the range of porters and particularly stouts increased. In 2013, there were 120 porters and 248 stouts available at the Great American Beer Festival, and there are many more out there turned out by brewers who did not enter the GABF, often brewed as specials or only on draft. New examples seem to pop up almost every day, so much so that it is impossible for me to list them all; instead, I have quoted a selection of these in the Definitions chapter, my choice of which is fairly arbitrary.

Interestingly, American craft brewers inspired those in Britain, and many of them followed this trend and put porter and/or stout on their list. Even some of the bigger brewers there were induced to brew a porter, both Guinness and Whitbread turning out their own version (Guinness, rather ironically, calling theirs Harwood's Porter Ale), though unfortunately that beer did not last for long. Nevertheless, *CAMRA's Good Beer Guide* included 102 porters and 171 stouts as of 2013, mostly from small brewers. But porter did come back to London when the regional family brewer Fuller's brought out their version, which is still being brewed today. Thus it could be argued that this very London brew had come full circle, via a sojourn in America! An interesting example to illustrate that is the rejuvenation of Courage's (once Barclay's) Imperial Russian Stout. Wells & Young bought the rights to the Courage brands from Scottish Courage, a conglomerate swallowed up by two behemoths, Heineken and Carlsberg. The new version was first brewed in May 2011 at 10% abv, and the head brewer, Jim Robertson, says he was one of the last to have brewed the beer in London, so it should be authentic. And where was it to be launched? Why, at the Falling Rock Tap House in Denver! But there has been another interesting development in the UK. In 2013, Elland 1872 Porter won the title of Supreme Champion Winter Beer of Britain, and followed

THE ANCHOR BREWHOUSE

In December 1787 the Aberdonian John Courage purchased a small brewhouse on this site. Little more than a year later the first entry in the brewing book records that John Courage had brewed 51 barrels of beer at the Anchor Brewhouse, Horselydown.

Three separate elements, Boilerhouse, Brewhouse and Malt Mill, each expressing different functions in the process of beer making, are united to form the Anchor Brewhouse's characterful and picturesque composition.

The building is an expression of historical continuity, for brewing on the river has always been an important feature of London's Thames-side. Brewing in Southwark is mentioned by Chaucer, and in Horselydown by Shakespeare.

The original part of this building dates from 1871 and was largely rebuilt in 1894-1895. Reconstructed, restored and refurbished in 1985-1989, it is now a Grade II listed building situated in the Tower Bridge Conservation Area.

Epitaph to one of the early porter breweries. Thrale's Anchor Brewery no longer exists, but it is commemorated with the above plaque, which sits behind the resurrected Globe Theater—that was the brainchild of an American, Sam Wanamaker!

that by being named Champion Beer of Britain. The 6.7% abv porter was brewed in Yorkshire to a recipe based on an 1872 porter, so porter rules in Britain again!

Just after I wrote the above, I received a press release from Marty Jones, then of Wynkoop Brewing in Denver, Colorado, announcing a new beer from Wynkoop. It came complete with label and video on YouTube, and was called Rocky Mountain Oyster Stout, made with bull's testicles, or Rocky Mountain Oysters. I was in Britain at the time, and due to the time lag it was actually the next day that I read the release. Only later did I find out it came out on April 1! American craft brewers not only brew good beer, but they also have a sense of humor!

CHAPTER TWO

PORTER AND STOUT DEFINITIONS

I HAVE DEALT WITH WHAT PORTER AND STOUT *WERE* LIKE; NOW we need to look at where they are today. Stouts and porters are British in origin, and there are now a healthy number of such beers being brewed by British craft brewers. Yet this is a recent phenomenon, and it was American craft brewers who led the way in bringing these styles out of the obscurity into which they had fallen in Britain (though not in Ireland). This is reflected in the fact that there are two major US organizations who literally "set the style" for beers, although principally for competition purposes. These are the Brewers Association (BA) and the Beer Judge Certification Program (BJCP), and their findings are available on their websites: www.brewersassociation.org and www.bjcp.org, respectively.

I do not intend to reproduce these copyrighted materials here, but rather to give you my own views as to what these beers are and how they should taste. Those views will include some criticism of the AHA and BJCP definitions, but I intend that to be

Rob Leonard, owner and brewer at the new New England Brewery, Woodbridge, Connecticut.

constructive and written in the sense that these are mere guidelines, and should not be regarded as restrictive when brewing your own beers. I should note here that I wrote the first book in the Brewers Association Classic Beer Styles series (*Pale Ale*), and followed that with the fifth (*Porter*), so I have played a significant part in defining styles in the United States. My definitions here will be largely descriptive, rather than based on numbers, although I shall give numbers where I consider them to be useful. I shall certainly give a descriptive view as to color in this section, because quoting SRM is of limited use in this case. Even porters are mostly above 20 SRM, and stouts are mostly at 40 SRM and above. Therefore, all these beers are dark to the eye (especially when in a pint glass), and it is the hue, rather than the absolute color, that is important. One figure I shall give is the ratio of IBU to original gravity (IBU/OG), where OG in this case is the original specific gravity x 1000. My reasoning is that this is more informative when talking about a range of IBU and OG, as we do in a definition, because to maintain a balance in the beer, the IBU level should generally increase proportionally as the OG increases.

In their respective 2013 schedules, the BJCP lists three porters (brown, robust, and Baltic), and six types of stout (dry, sweet, oatmeal, foreign extra, American, and Russian Imperial). The BJCP group puts smoked porter in the "Other Smoked Beer" category, while the BA lists smoked porter as a separate style. BA does not list Russian Imperial stout, and it is replaced by three categories: British-style and American-style Imperial stouts, and American-style Imperial porter. This is gilding the lily with a vengeance, as my simple mind sees it, because the parameters given for these show little difference from one another, except in levels of hop bitterness. And the high level of alcohol precludes Imperial porter from being a porter; it is simply a stout! So I would put them together as all being Imperial stout; we can drop the Russian bit, because that only derived from one English beer that was originally exported to Russia in the eighteenth century and was still being brewed in the late twentieth century. However, I should point out that there is a reason for including Imperial porter as a separate style, and that is because the early eighteenth-century porters would have been higher in alcohol than modern brown porter. So if you are trying to re-create such a beer, then are you justified in calling it "Imperial"? I don't think so, because the first exports of porters/stouts to Russia were made in the latter part of the eighteenth century, and the term "Imperial" was not added until around 1869. So a modern version of an eighteenth-century porter just cannot be called Imperial porter, even though it is too alcoholic to fit our modern definitions of brown porter! And I note that, for these styles, there was only one category in which prizes were awarded in the 2013 GABF competition, and that was labeled "Imperial Stout."

I do not accept smoked porter as a separate category. That is because there was likely a smoky flavor in at least some versions of the early London porters, so I see "smoke" as just another part of the brewer's palette when brewing a porter. I note that the Brewers Association Great American Beer Festival includes a separate category for wood- and barrel-aged strong stout, in addition to those already mentioned. I shall make some mention of such beers below, but I shall not treat them as separate from other stouts, because barrel aging is a post-brewing treatment and is not directly related to the brewing process.

I am therefore going to stick to considering the nine designations of brown, robust, and Baltic porters, along with dry, sweet, oatmeal, foreign extra, American, and Imperial stouts. Since most of them have demonstrable historical pedigrees (even the American stout), these categories are useful as a way of looking at these beers. However, they do not include every variety of porter available commercially (let alone those brewed at home). Fruit-flavored porters and stouts can be found, as well as those flavored with vanilla, chocolate, coffee, and even spices. Some even feature bourbon flavors, picked up from storage in whiskey casks. Style fanatics might put these beers into other categories, but I still regard them as porters, and they underline the fact that style definitions are only guidelines and should be used as such. You can stretch them however you like, and put whatever flavor you desire in your own beer. The ultimate standard for any beer is "Does it taste good?" If it does, the parameters to which it is brewed become unimportant. You only really have to follow the BA/BJCP parameters if you are submitting the beer in one of their sponsored competitions.

I am adhering to use of the term Baltic porter for convenience's sake, even though it is really too high in alcohol to be called a porter. But Baltic porter is unequivocally listed as a lager beer in the BA style guidelines, and it is true that commercial examples are bottom-fermented. Yet historically, they have developed from the Russian Imperial stouts exported by British brewers, which to my mind fits them in the porter/stout class of beers, be they lagers or not. Bear in mind that one of the most enduring American porters is that produced by Yuengling, with its roots going back to the early nineteenth century, and it is also bottom-fermented! And what about Imperial Extra Stout, brewed by the British company Harvey and Son, under license to A. LeCoq? LeCoq used to import such a beer to Russia from England, and was later permitted to use the "Imperial" designation. When supplies dried up, he eventually set up a brewery to produce his own version. This was in Estonia, so should this beer really be called Baltic stout? Perhaps then what we now call Baltic porters should be given the same designation? I do not throw this in just to confuse you, but merely to emphasize the fact that the BA/BJCP designations are, and can only be, guidelines.

Yet you cannot just cross the guidelines carelessly without causing havoc and confusion. Just as an example, a Pro/Am competition was held during the 2011 National Homebrewer's Conference. The September/October 2011 issue of *Zymurgy* gave the winner two designations on the same page, namely Imperial porter and robust porter. Since the recipe indicates the beer was at 9.3 percent, and the only high-roasted malt was chocolate, this cannot be a robust porter, and I have already called the game over on Imperial porter above. The beer was an Imperial stout, no more, no less.

These definitions may read as if I am disregarding extract brewing. That is not so, for I am simply describing what ingredients can be used for these beers. Those ingredients will be discussed in a later chapter, including how to use them in extract beers where appropriate. In chapter 5 on recipes, I shall give instructions for both all-grain and extract-based beers.

BROWN PORTER

This beer is the modern equivalent of the early porters, although it is not a match for them. It should be dark brown (not black) in color, preferably with a warm, reddish tint. Above all, it should be a well-balanced, easy-drinking beer with individual flavor notes blending in, rather than standing out. In particular, it should not display roasted flavors or high-hop bitterness, as these would respectively make it a robust porter or dry stout. If you use an English yeast strain, it may have a low level of fruity esters, and that is acceptable but should not be overdone, and diacetyl is probably not desirable.

It has to be below about 5.5% abv or it becomes a stout; that means an OG of around 1.055 (13.6°P) maximum. You can go as low as 1.035 (9.0°P) if you like, but you are then really treading in mild ale category. But note that the Brewers Association 2013 number for maximum % abv (6.0%) is much too high for the OG range given. As far as bittering hops go, I like to keep the IBU/OG ratio in the range around 0.6, which means an IBU level of 30 for an OG of 1.050 (12.4°P), for example. However, don't take that as dogma, for you can go higher, depending upon the malts used. And, of course, you are not restricted to which hop variety you use for bittering, so high alpha acid varieties are generally fine. This is not a beer that usually has noticeable hop character and/or aroma, but you are not bound by that convention if you feel you want those characteristics in your porter. In fact, I see that Real Ale Brewing of Blanco, Texas, has recently brought out Dry-Hopped Porter (5.7%), although I haven't been able to taste it and tell you what it is like.

I next have to mention Yuengling porter (4.7%) as the oldest US version of the style (although an oddball, in the sense of being bottom-fermented). One of the best examples I have come across is the porter from Back East brewing of Bloomfield, Connecticut; it is a little high alcohol at 6% abv, but has a balance that really exemplifies this style. Some other examples of brown porters available in the United States are Sierra Nevada Porter (5.6% abv); Deschutes Black Butte Porter at 5.2% abv, from Bend, Oregon; Geary's London Porter (4.2% abv) out of Portland, Maine; and Smuttynose Robust Porter from Portsmouth, New Hampshire, brewed at 5.7% abv. Yes, I know what the label says on the last one, but it drinks like a brown porter! Then there's Narragansett Porter out of little Rhode Island, a revival of the first porter I ever drank, and sold in cans. It is very smooth and well-balanced, and drinks like a brown porter, but is really too strong for the category at 7% abv. Left Hand Brewing Co. offers Black Jack Porter, a fine example, but again high in alcohol at 6.8% abv, while more reasonably, Stone has their Smoked Porter at 5.9% (with smoke barely noticeable). Cisco Brewers from Nantucket offers the very black Moor Porter (5.5% abv), while Martha's Exchange Restaurant and Brewery (Nashua, New Hampshire) offers Steeplechase Porter, also at 5.5% abv. From Deerfield, Massachusetts, Berkshire Brewing Co. has Drayman's Porter at the relatively high 6.2% abv, but very well-balanced and with a full, brown malt–type flavor. From Oxford, Connecticut, Cavalry Brewing Co. offers Big Wally Porter (4.8% abv), while Otter Creek (Middlebury, Vermont) has Stovepipe Porter (4.4% abv). A very pleasant brown porter comes from Widmer Brothers out of Portland, Oregon, weighing in at a rather high 6.0% abv and named Oatmeal Porter (no comment!).

Something worth mentioning from across the Atlantic is an excellent example of a brown porter from the home of the style: Fuller's London Porter (5.4% abv). Another London brew is Meantime Porter, which fits this category well, although at 6.5% abv it is somewhat higher in alcohol than demanded by the above definition, but since it is based on a 1750 recipe, it has more than a little credibility. Also worth a mention is St. Peter's Old-Style Porter from Suffolk in England (available on the United States East Coast, at least). It is intriguing because it is a blend of a young and an aged beer, which was the way porters were often blended in England in the eighteenth century. This approach gives it some of that very pleasant, raisin-like, vinous old ale flavor, yet at 5.1% abv, it is still very drinkable. Next, I have to include a rather unusual example, Master Thief Porter, which is pretty much only available in Colorado. It is produced by Grimm Brothers and brewed with de-husked malts, German hops, and fermented with alt yeast at 6.7% abv. Yes, it's a German porter! At first sight, this shoots down our attempts to completely define any style, doesn't it? Yet my memory tells me that the first time I tasted an alt (Remmer Bräu) in Germany, a lifetime ago, it was dark brown, lightly hopped, but malty and well-balanced, very much like a brown porter. So perhaps it's Grimm Brothers who have got it right, rather than us style mavens? Then again, there's Smoked Porter from Captain Lawrence Brewing Company (Elmsford, New York) at 45 IBU, and well over the top of the guidelines at an OG of 1.066 (16°P). The grains for this are German smoked, Munich, and Vienna malts with English pale and chocolate malts and English roast barley. I think there's a good point to be made here. It looks from the numbers that the brewer wanted to make something to approximate to the original eighteenth-century porters, but selected the grains according to the result he wanted to achieve. And that is always a good method for constructing a new recipe!

The modern "traditional" approach to brown porter is to use crystal and chocolate malts in the grist to provide both color and subtle

Do you remember, Tom, the Cottage
The Old Inn on the river's bank;
Where we ate many a savory pottage,
And many a cooling draught have drank,
And those three rustic signs together
Triangular that braved the gale
Through summer and through winter weather,
Proclaiming here was Taylor's ale?

A verse in praise of Taylor's Ale 1866—note the sign for Imperial Cream Ale!

nutty and chocolate notes, with no harshness. But you can also use brown malt to make it somewhat more authentic. Or you can try mixtures of pale, brown, and amber malts, as was common practice in the nineteenth century. There is an interesting new variation on brown malt produced by Briess. This is Carabrown® malt, which is produced to be on the light side of brown malt, and while delivering much of the flavor of English brown malt, it also has some of the characteristics of crystal malt and confers a little sweetness on the beer.

Other malts can play in this game, too; Belgian Special B, although technically a crystal malt, gives more of a toffee/caramel flavor than English crystal malt, and is much to my taste in a porter. Briess Special Roast and Belgian Biscuit malts also add interesting flavor notes in the toffee/caramel/bready/biscuit area. Don't overdo them—but properly handled, they can add more depth to this beer without disturbing its balance. I sometimes like to play around with base malts too, substituting some of the pale malt with Munich, Vienna, or Victory malts. In fact, you can make mild ale malt (Briess Ashburne Mild, for example) your base malt in place of pale malt to some advantage.

Then there's smoked malt, which obviously adds a smoky flavor that some people like. It can be overdone, so you do not want to use rauch malt, but a peated malt works well when used in moderation. The smoke flavor can throw the beer out of balance, and I remember tasting an Alaskan smoked porter at the GABF a few years ago that I found to be almost undrinkable. But a number of historians think that smoke flavor in a porter makes it authentic to the original, although I am not convinced of that. And for the record, note that Alaskan smoked porter does not fit the definition I gave above, for it is brewed to 6.5% abv—although it does match my IBU/OG ratio.

As an example of what can be done with this kind of beer, a couple of years ago I came across a beer in England—Entire Butt English Porter, brewed by the Salopian Brewing Co. at Shrewsbury in Shropshire, close to the border with North Wales. I did not list it above, because as far as I am aware, it is not available in the United States, and I mention it here only because of its unusual grain bill. This consisted of "fourteen different malts," namely Maris Otter pale, lager pale, wheat, pale crystal, dark crystal, pale chocolate, black, roast barley, caramalt, torrefied wheat, amber, brown, and malted oats. It is actually twelve malts, since torrefied wheat and roasted barley are not really malts, but I'm sure you get the picture anyway!

ROBUST PORTER

When black malt was invented in 1817, many British and Irish commercial brewers began using a proportion of it in their porter grist (although often still using brown and pale malts as well). Unwittingly, they had created a new sub-style of porter, sometimes known as Victorian porter, although our modern title is more informative. The results of this change are that robust porter tends to black, rather than red-black in color, and that it has a roasted malt flavor, which adds a "bite" or slight harshness to the beer's palate. This means that you can go a bit higher in hop bitterness, since that helps to offset the edge of the black malt and makes the beer more balanced. Like brown porter, some fruity estery notes (as might be expected from an English yeast strain) are appropriate. The presence of diacetyl is often thought to be inappropriate in this beer, but I find that low levels of this chemical can help to round out the flavor of a robust porter.

Again, I would aim at a maximum of 5.5% abv, but as always, there's some wiggle room here, and both BA and BJCP numbers are a little higher than this. As far as bittering levels go, I would opt for an IBU/OG ratio of around 0.7 to 0.8, which is a little higher than for brown porter. So for an OG of 1.052 (12.9°P), you would aim for about 42 IBU. As above, the bittering hop may be pretty much any high alpha acid variety that you happen to like. There really isn't any place for hop aroma or character in this beer, since it should be dominated (but not overwhelmed) by roasted malt flavors. However, some brewers do like hop flavor in their robust porter to balance any harshness from the black malt and do add hops late, or at the end of the boil.

If you want to try some robust porter, there's always the widely marketed 5.6% abv Anchor Porter, the first "new wave" porter, which appeared in the 1970s. Boulder Brewing's Planet Porter (5.5% abv) has also been around a while. Edmund Fitzgerald Porter (5.8%) (from Great Lakes Brewing in Ohio) and Odell's hoppy Cutthroat Porter (5.1% abv) (from Fort Collins, Colorado) are also good versions of this style, as are Flat12's Pogue's Run Porter from Indianapolis (5.5% abv) and Bell's 5.6% abv porter, brewed in Kalamazoo, Michigan. A West Coast brew, Perseus Porter, drinks well at 5.4% abv; on the other side of the country, we have Southern Tier Porter (from Lakewood, New York) at 5.8% abv, and out of Maine, Kennebunkport KBC Porter at 5.6% (which is actually brewed by Shipyard in Portland, Maine, and sold at Trader Joe's). Founder's Brewing Co. in Grand Rapids, Michigan, does a very good version at the somewhat high level of alcohol 6.5% abv. Boulevard Brewing has Bully Porter, with an IBU/OG ratio of 0.85 (5.4% abv), at the very top end of my definition, while Avery Brewing (Boulder, Colorado) does a robust porter called New World Porter, but out of the guidelines at 6.7% abv. A very well-balanced offering from California's Firestone Walker, Walker's Reserve Robust Porter at 5.9% abv, is brewed using some oat and barley flakes. Do we accept the brewer's designation of robust porter, or do we say it should really be an oatmeal stout, or do we invent a new style of oatmeal stout robust porter? I think the first, but this is another good example as to why we cannot be too rigid in setting parameters for a given style. In fact, just for good measure, Duck-Rabbit Brewing in North Carolina also does a robust porter (at the fairly high level of 5.7% abv) with oats added to the grist! A version made closer to home is Raincloud Porter made by Foolproof Brewing (Rhode Island), at the somewhat high level of 6.5% abv, and available in cans as well as bottles.

Many drinkers still love Taddy Porter (5.0% abv) from Samuel Smith in Yorkshire, England, which was an early arrival on these shores back in 1980 or so. Also from Britain (London's Greenwich area, to be precise) comes London Stout from Meantime Brewing, at 4.5% abv. Despite the name, I find it tastes more like a relatively modest robust porter. Also from across the pond, if you can find it, is Flag Porter (5.0%) from the Darwin Brewery, a beer originally formulated and made with a yeast sample recovered from a ship that sunk in the nineteenth century. And finally, there is the specialty draft offering of

Pre-Prohibition Porter at Willimantic Brewing's Main Street Café in Willimantic, Connecticut. It was a little high in alcohol at 5.9% abv for a robust porter, but was very well-balanced with a good body and definite (but modest) roast character. You'll see a recipe for this later on.

The simple approach to this beer is to use a base of 2-row pale malt with 2 to 5 percent black malt, but that should only be the beginning. A mixture of pale, brown, and black malts (perhaps also with some amber malt) could take you right back to the type of beer they were brewing in Early Victorian times. Carabrown® malt in place of English brown malt would suit this brew well. A more modern approach would be to use pale, crystal, and black malts, perhaps with a little chocolate malt to soften the roasted flavor. And don't be afraid to play around with different base malts, such as Munich, Vienna, and mild ale malts, as well as exploring the specialties such as Victory, Special B, and so on. As with brown porter, smoked malts can also be used in this style.

But there's another possibility you may well want to consider, and that is de-husked or debittered black malt. Briess has a new version of this called Blackprinz®, which has all the color of regular black malt and gives a good roasted, coffee-type flavor, but with little or none of the acrid flavor that can come from black malt. It can therefore be used in greater amounts, so as to intensify roast flavors without making the porter taste unduly harsh.

BALTIC PORTER

My remarks at the beginning of this chapter reflect the fact that the designation of this as a separate style is questionable, and that it could be regarded as a sub-style of Imperial stout rather than as a porter. It is seen by the BA as a lager style because commercial samples are brewed with a lager yeast strain, rather than with ale yeast. The virtually nationwide use of closed conical fermenters by craft and factory brewers means that the old distinction between top- and bottom-fermenting yeasts has largely disappeared. The distinction now is more that lager yeasts work at a lower temperature than ale yeasts, giving a slower fermentation and a smoother, cleaner flavor.

This style category has come into being as the result of an influx of examples being imported into North America in the last ten to fifteen years. These are brewed mainly in countries around the Baltic Sea (surprise!) and are often revivals or modern adaptations of old recipes for beers that had fallen out of fashion. In some countries, such as Poland, Russia, Lithuania, and Latvia, production of these types of beers had lapsed entirely under Communist rule, and only emerged again after the Berlin Wall and the Iron Curtain came down. As a matter of fact, in the USSR, it was almost impossible to find anything other than Czech imports at that time. What little was brewed in places like Russia and Ukraine was almost invariably produced on a Czech-designed plant, and more or less in the Pilsner style. You can take my word for it, as I spent a good deal of time in "closed" towns in the USSR. These were towns where "Westerners" were not allowed without special dispensation, and if you did go there, you were always under KGB scrutiny. Vodka was plentiful, but I seldom found any Russian beer worth drinking; that, of course, was in an earlier life!

The result of all this is that the so-called Baltic porter style is quite diffuse and covers a wide range in terms of alcohol content and flavor. I have in front of me a bottle of D. Carnegie Stark-Porter III (2001), with 5.5% abv (brewed by Carlsberg in Sweden, while a Polish sample is as high as 9.4% abv). I find that Baltic porters are often too sweet to my taste, but the better ones are quite satisfying. In fact, the 2001 Carnegie porter, ostensibly brewed to an 1836 recipe, has a nice rich aged beer flavor, and is more full-flavored than you might expect from a 5.5% beer (although more recently produced versions of it are just not as good). Chocolate flavors are often present in Baltic porters, but a strong roasted black malt taste should not be evident, and there should be no hint of diacetyl. As a result, these beers are often deep brown in color, rather than black. Hop bitterness is generally on the low side, and an IBU/OG ratio of around 0.4 to 0.5 is appropriate. While on the subject of flavor, I find the Carnegie porter most intriguing, for although it is only 5.5% abv, it has a full plummy, vinous flavor reminiscent of an English barley wine or strong old ale. This suggests to me that it could be a blend of an old and young beer, just as were some of the original porters. Or am I being blind to what is merely oxidation on aging?

This category was only introduced at the GABF some five years ago, so there are relatively few examples of it brewed in this country. A good American version of this style is Victory Baltic Thunder from Pennsylvania (8.5% abv), and Harpoon from Boston offers Leviathan Baltic Porter (9.5% abv), while the Colorado brewery Twisted Pine has their Pearl Street Porter in the Baltic style (6.7% abv). In 2010, Devil's Backbone Brewpub in Virginia won gold at the GABF with their "Danzig" offering in this category, at 8.0% abv and 25 IBU, and the 2011 winner was Battle Axe Baltic Porter (8% abv) from Fat Head's Brewery in Ohio. In my opinion, these and other American Baltic Porters are far better than those coming in from Eastern Europe, such as Black Boss (9.4% abv) and Okocim (8.3% abv) from Poland, or Aldaris (6.8% abv) from Latvia. Oh, and I have just noticed that the

Source: Author

The Twisted Pine brewery frontage in Boulder, Colorado; it looks like a craft brewery, doesn't it?

AC Golden Brewing Company (owned by you-know-who) had a Baltic porter at the 2011 GABF, but I didn't taste it, so I can't comment further.

Once you have decided what sort of OG suits your preference, brewing these beers is fairly straightforward—and much like for a brown porter, using 2-row pale or pilsner malt as the base. But you can use quite high proportions of Munich and Vienna, up to 50 percent of the grist for either or both together. These will help to give a non-roast complexity to the beer. For color, you can use a little chocolate malt, and crystal malts, as well as Special B, are prime candidates. There is a good argument for using a mix of crystal malts, say 2 to 3 percent (of the total grist) each of 40, 80, and 120°L grades so as to give sweetness, muted roast flavors, and red-brown color in the beer. Some brown malt (5 to 10 percent) may add a little extra licorice flavor, and even a tiny amount (1 to 2 percent) of de-husked black malt will help color and give a slight coffee flavor with no harshness. For the record, Zywiec Porter from Poland weighs in at 9.5% abv, and is reportedly brewed using pilsner, caramalt, Munich, and roasted malts, and hopped with German Magnum, Nugget, and Polish Taurus hops.

Above all, you will need to use a lager yeast strain (I'll make suggestions on particular strains later) and ferment at low temperatures. By which I mean a primary at 45°F to 55°F (7°C to 13°C), and this must be followed by a day or two at around 65°F (18°C) to remove diacetyl. Lagering for a period at lower temperatures, say around 35°F (2°C), will help to ensure that the beer is smooth and clean in flavor.

DRY STOUT

This style is sometimes billed as "Classic Irish," since it is primarily based on Guinness Stout and is a step on from robust porter, with an extra bite added by the use of roasted barley. It is not clear when Guinness first started using this grain, and there are plenty of myths about it being discovered as a good ingredient after an accidental charring of the grain. The more likely, but also more prosaic, explanation is that British and Irish brewers experimented with using raw barley as a cheap substitute for pale malt around the late nineteenth to early twentieth centuries. At that time it wasn't a particularly successful experiment, so the obvious next step was to try roasting it, and to use the product in stout brewing. Most modern commercial dry stouts are brewed with at least some roasted barley.

Dry stout has a reputation much higher than its quality warrants, largely due to some very clever marketing by Guinness. But it is really a modest session beer, for it can be as low as 3.8%, and should not be above about 5% (for competition purposes). Color is obviously quite black, though not intensely so, from the use of high-roast malts. Since black malt and roasted barley give a harsh and acrid flavor, this is often balanced by a relatively high hop bitterness level. An IBU/OG ratio of around 0.8 to 0.9 is quite common for this beer, which seldom if ever exhibits anything in the way of hop aroma or character. BA and BJCP definitions exclude the presence of diacetyl, but it seems to me that a moderate level actually adds something to this stout, which otherwise tends to be quite one-dimensional. Guinness is often said to add a flavor extract, the composition of which has never been publicly revealed. This is intended to add some of the characteristics of aged stout—including acidity—to the finished product, and to make it more complex. I for one find it unnoticeable in a low-gravity beer dominated by roasted barley, and I suspect that the perpetrators of this rumor have assumed that because this flavor extract *is* added to Foreign Extra Stout, it must also be added to the lesser regular stout. Formation of a good tight head is held to be very important in this beer, but this is a function of the dispense method, and is only partly due to brewing procedures. Indeed, I think the tight head produced by a Guinness-style faucet and nitrogen gas dispenser is a good way to ensure that this beer is not one-dimensional.

There aren't many commercial examples of dry stout with wide distribution here, perhaps for the obvious reason that they would be competing directly with Guinness. Of course, Guinness is not the only Irish stout, for the Heineken brands from Cork, Murphy's (4.0% abv), and Beamish (4.1% abv) are of comparable quality to Guinness. Note that the strength of Guinness Stout (excluding Foreign Extra Stout) varies according to where it is sold; in the United States, Guinness

Draught is 4.2% abv, while Guinness Extra weighs in at 5.0% abv, although both figures might have changed by the time you read this! There are still some good dry stouts brewed in England, and one that makes it over here is Dorothy Goodbody Stout (4.6%, from Wye Valley Brewery in Herefordshire). In the United States, the style seems to be more common in brewpubs than in packaging breweries. A few I would offer include Moylan's Dry Irish Stout from Moylan's Brewery in Novato, California (5.0% abv); Rubicon Irish Stout from Rubicon Brewing Company in Sacramento, California (4.8% abv), and served under nitrogen; and McLuhr's Irish Stout from Dillon Dam Brewing in Dillon, Colorado, also served under nitrogen. The Devil's Backbone Brewpub in Virginia offers Ramsey's Draft at 4.2% abv, which is dispensed using nitrogen. Blue Fin Stout (4.7% abv) from Shipyard Brewing (Portland, Maine) is only described as "classic Irish stout" on its website, and not on the bottle label.

Classic dry stout recipes use a pale malt base, along with 10 percent roasted and 30 percent flaked barley, the latter supposedly as an aid to head retention. In fact, Guinness no longer uses flaked barley, since with modern milling methods, they are able to use straight raw barley instead. There is a good argument for substituting some of these grains with black and/or chocolate malts, with the latter especially leading to a somewhat creamier flavor. You have to be careful, though, or you will be straying into the robust porter category if you don't have at least some roasted barley flavor in the beer. As with brown and robust porters, this beer can benefit from including one or more specialty malts, such as brown, Special B, crystal, and so on. I like to include some Victory malt (up to 20 percent, depending upon the other components), as this adds some nuttiness, which seems to suit this stout well.

A common mistake in brewing this style of beer is to overdo the roasted malts so that the result is an overly acidic beer. This can be particularly noticeable if your brewing water contains little in the way of bicarbonate ions. These have the capacity to buffer or dampen the effect of the roasted malt, so as to prevent the pH of the beer from falling too far and giving it a harsh and acrid nature, rather than a pleasant roastiness. I shall discuss that further in chapter 3.

Yeast, as always, plays an important part here, and you do want a strain giving good attenuation (65 to 75 percent), so that the beer is quite dry and not sweet. Both suppliers of liquid yeasts, Wyeast and White Labs offer an Irish Ale strain that works well. These will produce that low level of diacetyl I discussed above. If you are one of those few who like diacetyl flavor, then the Ringwood strain can be counted on to do just that.

Finally, if you want that fine, tight head on your stout when serving it on draught, you can easily obtain a stout faucet from homebrew suppliers. In order to realize your Irish Ideal of a full, tight head of small bubbles, you should use either nitrogen or a nitrogen/carbon dioxide mix. That will be discussed in more detail in chapter 5. However, you might feel, as I do, that this is an unnecessary expense, and that the more important thing is to brew a flavorful and interesting beer.

Finally, finally, a commercial seen in a pub stated, "Over seven million Guinnesses are drunk every day," which prompted the reply, "Didn't know it was such a large family."

SWEET STOUT

A comparatively simple beer, sometimes also called cream stout or milk stout, it is something of an elusive style. It is English in origin, but up until the 1970s, there were only one or two examples being brewed there, with the only one of any consequence being Mackeson Stout, although other versions of the beer were still being produced in the Caribbean and in Malta. The upsurge in craft brewing in Britain seems to have produced only one or two sweet stouts. But American craft brewers, with their usual urge to experiment, have come up with several versions of the beer, often made with some modifications of the so-called "classic" sweet stout.

It was originally called "milk stout" because it relied on the addition of lactose, a sugar that yeast does not ferment and which gives a fullness of palate to the beer, while it remains relatively low in alcohol. The food police banned the use of "milk" in the name around the 1940s, and it became just "stout" or "extra stout." The addition of "cream" or "sweet" to the category came about later, in a somewhat random manner, until the latter usage was formalized by the BA/BJCP classifications.

The beer is sweet, though less so than you might expect, since lactose gives only about 40 percent of the sweetness of a similar concentration of sucrose. Exactly how sweet your stout is going to be depends upon how much lactose you use, of course; a common figure is about 2 to 3 percent by weight in the finished beer, which is about 1 pound in 5 US gallons (19L). As a dissolved solid, it contributes to the specific gravity of wort and beer, and as a sugar, 1 percent lactose corresponds roughly with 1.004 SG (1°P). So 3 percent lactose gives approximately 1.012 SG. Therefore, a sweet stout containing 3 percent lactose and with OG 1.042, in terms of fermentable solids has an OG of only 1.030, and will only ferment out to about 2.8 to 3.0% abv at most.

The result of all this is that the guidelines for this beer are somewhat vague. Alcohol content can vary from 3.0% abv to over 5% abv, although OG can range from around 1.040 to as much as 1.065. The IBU/OG ratio doesn't work well in this case, but hop bitterness should be low, say 15 to 30 IBU. Much of the color will come from roasted malts, so the beer will be deep brown to black. Sweet stouts can be exactly that, with sweetness dominant and the beer rather bland; a well-brewed one will have plenty of fullness and mouthfeel without being too sweet, so that it is properly balanced.

It is really a niche product, but there are a number of sweet stouts around, such as Samuel Adams Cream Stout (4.9% abv) from the Boston Beer Company. One I enjoyed very much at the brewery is Milk Stout from Left Hand Brewing Company in Longmont, Colorado, although at 6% abv, it is over the guideline limit. Intriguingly, its grain bill includes both flaked oats and flaked barley, so perhaps it should be called milk dry oatmeal stout? Duck-Rabbit from North Carolina (whom I mentioned earlier for their robust porter) also offers the simplistically titled but very pleasant Duck-Rabbit Milk Stout (5.7% abv), while Wynkoop Brewing Co. in Denver serves up Cowtown Milk Stout at 4.8% abv. The curiously named Yak & Yeti

Brewpub in Denver has its Chai Milk Stout at 5.7% abv, with added chai spice. Another variation comes from Odell Brewing in Fort Collins, Colorado; this is made with milk chocolate as well as lactose, and is touted as being as high as 8.5% abv. You might also want to look out for the curiously named Buffalo Sweat (5.0% abv) from Tall Grass Brewing of Manhattan, Kansas; Dark Horse Brewing's Too Cream Stout of Marshall, Michigan, at the very high level of 7% abv; and Milk Stout from Lancaster Brewing Co. in Lancaster, Pennsylvania. The latter contains 5.3% abv and is hopped with Goldings, as well as that old craft brewer's favorite, Cascade. Two East Coast examples are the excellent Mother's Milk (6.7% abv, from Keegan's Ales in Saratoga Springs, New York), and Fat-Ten-Er #3 Milk Stout (5.5% abv, from New England Brewing in Woodbridge, Connecticut). One that muddies the style definition is Oatmeal Milk Stout (6.7%) from River Horse Brewing Co. in Lambertville, New Jersey. Southern Tier Brewing Co. (Lakewood, New York) really throws a monkey wrench among the pigeons with their Crème Brûlée Stout, which they designate as an Imperial milk stout on their website. At 9.6% abv and sweetened with lactose, that seems to be right, except for the minor detail that there is no official Imperial milk stout category. A further complication is that it is brewed with vanilla beans, so perhaps it should just come under the heading of flavored stout? You could argue that the term Imperial milk stout is more or less self-explanatory, so it's okay if that's what the brewers want to call it. Unfortunately, they drop the word "milk" on the main face of the label, and mention the presence of lactose only on its side. So what should it really be called? Does it matter? Or shall we just have another one while we think about it?

Apart from the base pale malt, almost all bets are off as far as other malts are concerned. Munich and Vienna malts, crystal, chocolate, and black malts, and even oats (malted or otherwise) will all add something to this beer. Modern American examples often use roasted barley, since its rather harsh flavor will nicely balance the sweetness of the beer. I think 2 to 3 percent lactose by weight is about right; more will make the beer too cloying, but you could go a bit higher if the "non-lactose gravity" is as high as 1.055 (13.6°P) or more. You might also want to explore the possibility of producing this beer with little or no lactose, but with significant amounts (15 to 20 percent of the grist) of caramel malts, some brown malt, and mash at relatively high temperatures (about 156°F or 69°C) so as to increase dextrin levels in the beer. If you do that, you want to avoid roasted barley and use chocolate malt and/or de-husked black malt to keep the flavor mellow.

FOREIGN EXTRA STOUT

This style derives (like dry stout) from a Guinness beer of the same name. It started life as a porter, the first West India Porter being brewed in 1801, using only pale and brown malts. As nomenclature changed and black malt was introduced to the brewing process, West India Porter morphed into Double Stout Foreign and then Foreign Extra Stout, with a product under this name still in production by Guinness. Stouts produced in Jamaica (Dragon) and Trinidad (Lion) have been quoted by some as fitting this category, but to my mind, they are too sweet for that and should be classed as sweet stouts. The BJCP perception of this style is that it is very broad in terms of the range of sweetness to bitterness, while the BA definition requires noticeable roasted flavors and bitterness.

My approach to this is that Guinness Foreign Extra Stout is the exemplar of this style and our definitions flow from this, although there is one problem about doing so that I shall discuss later. If you accept this thesis, then this beer should have a black color and a definite roast malt flavor from the use of roasted barley and/or black malt. It should also have some malty sweetness, since it is a full-bodied, moderately strong drink at up to 7.5% abv (which is exactly what Guinness Foreign Extra weighs in at today), so that this style corresponds to that with OG of 1.070 to 1.075 (17 to 18.2°P). Hop bitterness should be noticeable, with an IBU/OG ratio of around 1.0, but hop character and aroma are not required. Again, our two authorities consider that diacetyl should not be noticeable in this beer, but I think a modest amount can help to balance the bitter and roasted flavors and give the beer a little more depth.

This is not a beer sold everywhere, and as far as I know there are no examples with widespread sales over the whole country. In this case, that is not because Guinness has an established position in this country, for Diageo did not sell Guinness Foreign Extra Stout in the United States until 2010. For the record, the medal winners in this category at the 2011 GABF Competition were: Dark Side Stout (6.4% abv) of Silver Moon Brewing in Bend, Oregon; Malpais Stout (7.0% abv) of La Cumbre Brewing Co. in Albuquerque, New Mexico; and Z-Man Stout (7.2% abv) of Pizza Port Ocean Beach in San Diego, California, although this beer is absent from the company's website. Left Hand Brewing Company, a standalone brewery, won the gold medal for this style at the 2010 GABF Competition with Fade to Black Vol.1 at 8.5% abv. But there is some overlap of this style with other high-gravity stouts, and there may be beers out there that fit this category, but have simply been designated as "stout" by the brewer.

So it is clear that, apart from the base pale malt, you need to use some roasted barley (up to 10 percent of the grist), but this can also be a mixture of roasted barley and black malt. If you want to add a little chocolate malt, that's fine, but use it in addition to the higher roasted malts. Some crystal malt or Belgian Special B can be used to advantage to balance the harshness with some sweetness and add a touch of caramel flavor, but should not be overdone. As always in a stout, a little brown malt adds a nice licorice touch, too. However, I don't think you should play around with specialty malts too much, for this is really an austere beer in which roasted and bitter notes should dominate.

The problem with Guinness Foreign Extra Stout that I referred to earlier is that it always has a definite sour note from the presence of lactic acid, and still does have a definite "bite" in its modern version. Originally, that arose from long storage in wooden vats before shipping abroad from Dublin. In the latter half of the twentieth century, Guinness changed its process and developed a method of making a concentrate that could be added to the beer in small amounts (2 to 3 percent) so as to add the aged beer flavor. The exact nature of this concentrate is proprietary, but the effect is that the beer tastes as if it had some of the character usually conferred by the *Brettanomyces* yeast strain. BJCP suggests that stout that has been treated with *Brettanomyces* is best not entered in the Foreign Extra Stout competition category, but should be entered in the Specialty Beer category. In other words, the Guinness version of this style, *on which the style is based,* does not even fit the style! Well, for my money, it absolutely does fit the style, and if you want to make a "Brett" version of Foreign Extra, you have my blessing to do so.

OATMEAL STOUT

I have said I am not sure that this should be a separate category, because when it appeared in England in the twentieth century, it seemed to me that it was little more than a name used by brewers to differentiate it from other producers' stouts. However, since oatmeal stouts virtually disappeared in England around the 1960s, stouts brewed with oats have become an American phenomenon as our craft and homebrewers expanded their horizons. And in that sense, I have to admit that these beers do deserve a category of their own.

If you check out the BA and BJCP guidelines on oatmeal stout, you will find that there is quite a bit of difference between them as to what the OG range should be (although abv levels are similar). Some of the flavor descriptions are also contradictory, perhaps reflecting the fact that because there is no clear pedigree for this stout, no one is quite sure as to exactly where this beer fits in on the black end of our beer spectrum.

Oatmeal stout can be seen as a sweet stout with oats in place of lactose, or as just filling the gap between sweet and dry stouts. Whatever the case may be, I think the keyword is modest, and that this beer should be smooth, in part thanks to the use of oats. It should also have a fair amount of body, so that it has good fullness on the palate. Roast flavors should be present, but fairly subtly so, which means that chocolate and de-husked black malt are a better option than regular black malt or roasted barley, although a touch of these latter can be used. This beer is generally dark brown to black in color, and abv can range from 4 percent to as high as 6 percent. You do not want much hop bitterness, or it will swamp the silkiness of texture given by the oats; I think an IBU/OG ratio of around 0.6 to 0.7 is appropriate. I go along with the BA/BJCP idea that this brew should not have noticeable levels of diacetyl.

Note that there is some debate about the use of oats/oat malt, and whether it materially affects beer flavor. Many brewers argue that this grain imparts a unique silky smoothness to the brew, while others say that the grain doesn't really do much at all, and that the smoothness of such beers merely reflects their brewing process. I am inclined to agree with the former view, though I still retain some skepticism about it. Perhaps that is because I cannot forget the words of Dr. Samuel Johnson, the great lexicographer, who defined oats as "a grain, which in England is generally given to horses, but in Scotland supports the people."

This is a style that is most often brewed as a one-off or as a special that may not be available at all times. There are one or two worth mentioning, such as 825 State Stout (6.0% abv) from Epic Brewing Company in Salt Lake City, Utah. Oatis Oatmeal Stout, brewed by Ninkasi Brewing Company at 7.2% abv in Eugene, Oregon, is said to be on sale year-round, as is Double Plow Oatmeal Stout (at 5.2% abv) from the Tractor Brewing Company in Los Lunas, New Mexico. A version of this beer that I enjoyed was Breckenridge's Oatmeal Stout from Denver, Colorado, at 4.95% abv, which edges towards dryness, since it is made with roasted barley as well as black and chocolate malts. Another version, Wolaver's Oatmeal Stout at 5.9% abv, comes from Otter Creek Brewing in Middlebury, Vermont. Ipswich Oatmeal Stout from Mercury Brewing Co. in Ipswich, Massachusetts, is at the very top end of the alcohol range at 6.8%, while Samuel Smith from Yorkshire in England offers a very smooth, lighter version at 5.0% abv. There are some Imperial oatmeal stouts that I shall mention under the Imperial stout category. That makes me ask the question: "If you take a recipe for imperial stout and brew it with added oatmeal, is it an imperial stout or an oatmeal stout?" Which leads back to the question: "If it tastes really good, does its name matter?"

As always, other malts can be used to produce this beer, especially if you want it to have some sweetness. That can be achieved in part by mashing at higher temperatures (154°F to 156°F, or 68°C to 69°C), but is better done with the addition of some CARAFA or crystal malts to the grist. Our old friends Special B, Victory malt, and brown malts can also suit this brew, and there is a good case for using a little Melanoidin malt to give it a little more palate fullness.

AMERICAN STOUT

Stouts were brewed in North America both before and after Prohibition, but here we are, talking about a style pretty much invented by US craft brewers in recent times. It does not have a long history, going back no further than 1978 at most, when New Albion started up and had a stout in its line-up. In the main, this style is defined by hops, as you might expect from the love and wonder that American craft brewers have for the hop. This beer should have significant bitterness and a noticeable hop flavor, the latter of which should come from citrusy or piney American hops varieties.

American stout should be a medium style of beer in terms of alcohol, with an OG of up to 1.075 (18.2°P), and 4.8 to 7.5% abv (BA again gives abv figures much higher than are likely to be achieved from the quoted OG). Bitterness is relatively high, with an IBU/OG ratio of around 1.0, and hop flavor should be present from late hop addition with American varieties such as Cascade, Chinook, Amarillo, Simcoe, although some brewers like the woody, earthy Northern Brewer variety. This beer should be a very dark brown to black in color and should have a distinct roasted coffee flavor that is not crowded out by the hop bitterness. The anti-diacetyl religion so prevalent in the United States dictates that there should be no butterscotch flavor in American stout. However, some sweetness may be tasted underneath the hop bitterness and roasted flavors.

Representative of this style are Kalamazoo Stout (6.0% abv) made by Bell's Brewery Inc. in Galesburg, Michigan, and the prize-winning Shakespeare Oatmeal Stout (6.5% abv), out of Rogue Ales in Newport, Oregon. Yes, I know what you're thinking when you see "oatmeal," but it won a bronze medal in the American-Style Stout category in the 2010 GABF Competition. Also a medalist in 2010 and 2011 was Disorder Stout from Barley Brown's Brewpub in Baker City, Oregon. Lake Trout Stout from Sebago Brewing Co. (Gorham, Maine) at 5.8% abv and 32 IBU seems a little low in IBU for the style, but it tastes more bitter than you would expect from the numbers. Avery Brewing Co. (Boulder, Colorado) produces Out of Bounds Stout, which is more aggressively hopped at 51 IBU, 6.3% abv. There is also Big Black Stout at 6% abv from 10 Barrel Brewing (Bend, Oregon), and there's usually always Damn Good Stout (6% abv) on tap at BrüRm@BAR in New Haven, Connecticut. Long Trail out of Vermont offers their Imperial Porter (8.3% abv), whose hop bitterness and character makes me consider it to be an American stout despite its high alcohol content.

So we know from the above that the brew needs hops, and will also need some high-roasted malt, such as black or chocolate. Roasted barley, of course, is well suited to this style. You can go a little higher with the roast flavor than for Foreign Extra Stout—say, a total of 10 to 12 percent of the grist using, for example, a mixture of chocolate and black, or chocolate and roasted barley. You should use a little crystal malt or Special B (perhaps as much as 5 percent of the total) for that little touch of background sweetness. Use Munich malt as a base, along with pale malt (about a 40:60 mix), to add a little bit of chewy mouthfeel. The use of brown malt for this style is not widespread amongst American craft brewers, but it could add licorice notes to this beer if you wanted to try it. Oat malt, flaked oats, or even rye malt could also be incorporated in the grist. American stout is one of the best styles produced by craft brewers, and because it has such a short history, it can be regarded as still in the experimental stage of development. Therefore, you can try any malt you like with it, even smoked or peated malt if that takes your fancy—just don't overdo it! Let the roast malts and hops stand out.

IMPERIAL STOUT

If you look at the BJCP guidelines for this style, you can easily become confused, for these indicate that this beer can have almost any characteristic, so long as it is big and has enough roasted malt flavor to make it a stout. The BA guidelines attempt to clarify this by introducing the further complication of having three categories: British-style Imperial stout, American-style Imperial stout, and American-style Imperial porter. Why do we need to call it American-style when there is no other Imperial porter category? You already know what I think of the latter "style" anyway, so let's move on.

When the London porter brewers first started shipping to Russia in the eighteenth century, they sent their strongest beers. By then they were often being called "stout," "stout porter," "brown stout," and various other combinations of these terms. So these first "Imperial stouts" were brewed with brown malt, since black malt had not yet arrived on the scene. That was to come in the next century, when it was readily adopted as a flavoring malt for stout.

So Imperial stout can have a little or a lot of roasted malt flavor. It can have chocolate, coffee, caramel, toasty, bready, and fruity flavors. Since the style virtually died out in Britain and has been revived by American craft brewers, it can have medium to high hop bitterness as well as hop flavor and aroma. It is usually very dark brown to black in color, and is generally brewed to OG 1.080 to 1.120 (19.3 to 28°P), much like the range for a barley wine. It should be fairly well attenuated, with a finishing gravity about 25 percent of OG, so that alcohol levels are in the range of 8 to 12% abv. As far as hopping rates go, the beer's IBU/OG ratio can be anywhere from 0.5 to 1.0; 80 to 90 IBU is about the maximum bittering you want and should only apply to beers at the high end of the OG range. Conventional wisdom says that diacetyl should not be present, but surely a modest amount will only add to the complexity of a big beer like this?

It will come as no surprise to you that despite (or because of) the fact that Imperial stouts are big beers, there are quite a few of them out there. Sitting right beside me are three of them, in no particular order: Imperial Stout (8.2% abv) from Lagunitas Brewing Co. of Petaluma, California, and The Czar Imperial Stout (11.03% abv) out of Avery Brewing Co. in Boulder, Colorado. I have Oat, an Imperial oatmeal stout (11.0%) from Southern Tier Brewing Company in Lakewood,

New York, as well as The Dogfather Imperial Stout (10% abv) produced by Laughing Dog Brewery in Ponderay, Idaho. A longtime favorite is the 9% abv Old Rasputin Russian Imperial Stout made by North Coast Brewing Co. of Fort Bragg, California. Great Divide from Denver, Colorado, has the excellent Yeti Imperial Stout (9.5% abv), of which there is also a chocolate oak-aged version. From SKA Brewing (Durango, Colorado) comes Nefarious Ten Pin Imperial Porter at 8% abv, and Northstar Imperial Porter (9% abv) is brewed by Twisted Pine in Boulder, Colorado. Cigar City Brewing (Tampa, Florida) produces several versions of this style, all around 10% abv (see under "Flavored Porters and Stouts"). Sierra Nevada (Chico, California) has Narwhal at 10.2% abv, while from Portland, Maine, comes Shipyard Brewing Co.'s Imperial Porter at 7.1% abv. Widmer Brothers in the other Portland (Oregon) recently launched KGB Russian Imperial Stout (9.2% abv), for which there are also raspberry and chocolate versions. Then there's an old favorite—Storm King Imperial Stout from Victory Brewing in Downingtown, Pennsylvania. It's 9.1% abv, but has enough hop character and bitterness to make it a well-balanced beer.

Closer to my home, there is Southampton Imperial Porter (7.2% abv) from Long Island; Port Jeff Brewing Company (also on Long Island) has a porter (7.5% abv) aged three months in a bourbon barrel, while Brooklyn Brewery in New York does Brooklyn Black Chocolate Stout, which I would put in the Imperial category at 10.0% abv. It is interesting in that it is not made with actual chocolate, yet tastes as though it has been, having been brewed with chocolate and black malts. From Matt Brewing in Utica, New York, we have the very creditable Saranac Imperial Stout at 9.0% abv, and New England Brewing in Woodbridge, Connecticut, makes their seasonal Imperial Stout Trooper (8.5%), which is an excellent example of the style. Thomas Hooker from Bloomfield, Connecticut, has an Imperial porter that is at around 8% abv; since it is brewed with flavor and aroma hops, it could even be held to fit in the American stout category. Bittering and flavor hops are a combination of Northern Brewer and the high alpha acid Zeus, but Hallertauer are used for aroma. From my hometown, we have Igor's Dream at 10.9% abv, brewed at Two Roads Brewery in Stratford, Connecticut, with the name referring to Igor Sikorsky, founder of the eponymous Stratford-based helicopter company, who was of Russian origin.

You should have no difficulty finding other versions of this style in your own area. Harvey's from Sussex in England have their A. LeCoq Imperial Extra Double Stout available here; it is made to match those early Russian Imperial stouts. It may do, but the bottle is actually corked, not capped, and every sample I have tried has had a sourness that I am sure the brewers did not intend. On the other hand, that perennial import from Tadcaster, Yorkshire, Samuel Smith's Imperial Stout (OG 1.070, 17°P, 7.0% abv), while full-bodied and pleasant, has a little "aged" flavor (in my sample) that may indicate slight oxidation, although many do not consider it to be a fault in this style of beer. An extreme for this style is Bourbon County Brand Stout from Goose Island (Chicago, Illinois), a barrel-aged beer at no less than 14.5% abv. And I conclude with another American beer, which I put here because I don't know where else to put it, as it does not really fit any category. That is Dogfish Head World Wide Stout, which has 70 IBU and varies in alcohol (it is an occasional brew) from 15 to 20%. It takes special techniques to brew such a beer, and frankly I do not think it is worth it, as I found my sample of it to be cloyingly sweet.

There may be many Imperial stouts produced in the United States, but apart from those cited above, few British brewers offer beers that would fit this category. However, I must mention here an interesting experiment involving a number of English brewers and organized by Tim O'Rourke of Brilliant Beer. Briefly, the brewers were invited to brew a version of Russian Imperial stout, and these were then shipped on a clipper sailboat to Russia, as were the original versions of this style. Around the Baltic, the ship presented its cargo at beer festivals in Copenhagen, Stockholm, Helsinki, and finally in St. Petersburg. The list of brewers, which includes some well-known names, was: All Gates Brewery, Bartrams, Black Sheep, Dark Star Brewery, Elgood Brewery, Fuller, Harvey Brewery, Meantime, Shepherd Neame, St. Austell Brewery, Thornbridge, Wadworth Brewery, William Worthington Brewery, and Wye Valley Brewery. The bad news is that many of these beers were one-offs, and may not be brewed for general release, but it could be worth your while to keep an eye open for them in case any of them should appear on store shelves over here.

And finally, one British version of this style that *is* sold over here is the aforementioned Courage Russian Imperial Stout at 10% abv. This is really the epitome of the style and is now brewed by Wells & Young's Brewing Co. It was originally brewed by Barclay, Perkins and Co. in the late eighteenth century, until that brewery was taken over by Courage & Co. in 1955, and Courage itself passed through several hands before the brands ended up at Wells & Young's.

Clearly you have a lot of wiggle room when it comes to brewing Imperial stout. The base, as usual, should be a 2-row pale malt, with roast malts such as brown, chocolate, and black malts, or roasted barley, in any combination you like. A good combination for me would be 80 percent pale malt, 10 percent brown malt, plus 5 percent chocolate and 5 percent black malt. An interesting approach would be to substitute the chocolate malt with chocolate wheat or rye for some extra complexity. But you could also include crystal and caramel malts to good effect, especially the more highly colored ones. As far as hops go, you can use whatever you like for bittering; since you are going for fairly high bitterness levels, high alpha acid varieties such as Centennial, Columbus, Magnum, and Northern Brewer, or the newer Mosaic are best because of the smaller amount required. For hop flavor and aroma, you again have a wide choice; because of the beer's origin, English hops such as Fuggles and Goldings are good, but their effect will be subdued in such a big beer. With

Two bottles from Courage that once sat in my beer cellar and were drunk long ago.

American hops, choose whichever variety you like best, either a citrusy, piney, or floral character. But don't overdo the hop flavor, because this beer should be chiefly about the malt and various roasted malts. You will need a yeast strain that gives good attenuation, and you can go for the clean flavor of the Californian Ale yeast, or the London Ale strain offered by both Wyeast and White Labs.

FLAVORED PORTERS AND STOUTS

These beers do not form a separate, clearly defined category, and I never intended to include them in this chapter. However, American craft and homebrewers are always experimenting and pushing the envelope, as I found at the 2011 Great American Beer Festival. There were coffee, chocolate, vanilla, coconut, wild cherry, pecan, peanut butter, and bourbon-flavored porters. In the stouts, there were coffee and chocolate examples again, along with coconut, cherry, blueberry-oatmeal, chocolate-chipotle, and even a Belgian stout!

So there is obvious interest in brewing these kinds of beer, and I thought I should discuss them a little here. There are no ground rules, so I am just going to make a few suggestions. First of all, think very carefully as to what kind of base porter or stout is likely to work best with the flavoring in which you are interested. It is very easy to drown out the beer flavor and leave you with nothing but an alcoholic fruit drink! I once tasted a chocolate porter made by a well-respected English brewer, and all it tasted of was chocolate syrup; no beer flavor whatsoever. And an American blackberry porter I had recently was very pleasant—if you like blackberry cordial, that is. So secondly, be sure that you are not adding an unnecessary flavor to a beer, such as an Imperial stout, that is already bursting with flavor at every corner.

But it is no surprise that both coffee and chocolate go well with porters and stouts, since they add flavors that marry well with those from the roasted malts used to brew the beer. Rogue Ales (Newport, Oregon) has its Chocolate Stout (6.5% abv, the same as for its Shakespeare Oatmeal Stout) and also a Mocha Porter (5.5% abv). Lagunitas (Petaluma, California) has a Cappuccino Stout (8.3% abv), and Great

Divide (Denver, Colorado) offers their chocolate oak-aged Yeti Imperial Stout (9.5% abv) as well as an espresso oak-aged Yeti version at the same strength. Wolaver's Alta Gracia Coffee Porter (5.0% abv) from Otter Creek in Middlebury, Vermont, is a very well-balanced beer, while Sea Dog from Portland, Maine, produces a 5.6% abv Hazelnut Porter, whose flavor I found a little strange, but quite pleasant. BrüRm@ BAR in New Haven, Connecticut—where I have been known to help out—brews a very nice Espresso Coffee Stout (6.6% abv). Berkshire Brewing Co. (Deerfield, Massachusetts) makes a brew called Dean's Beans Coffeehouse Porter, brewed to the same strength (6.2% abv, 36 IBU) as their Drayman's Porter. In this case, I find that the coffee flavor improves the beer by giving it a drier edge and reducing its apparent sweetness. Dogfish Head (Milton, Delaware) offers a chicory stout (5.2% abv), using roasted chicory as well as coffee in the ingredients.

Vanilla also goes very well with a brown porter in particular, adding a clean, smooth flavor to meld with the taste from chocolate malt. The Vanilla Porter (4.7%, 16 IBU) from the Breckenridge Brewpub in Denver, Colorado, is a very pleasant example I tried not long ago at the brewpub, and Southern Tier (Lakewood, New York) does their vanilla-flavored Crème Brûlée Imperial Stout, which I have already referred to under the Sweet Stout section. I'll provide recipes for beers using coffee, chocolate, and vanilla later on. American brewers are fonder of this category than those in the UK, although there are one or two examples brewed over there. The best, and one that can be found over here, is Young's Double Chocolate Stout (5.2% abv). I have to mention it because it was a beer beloved by Tom Schrader, a brewing buddy of mine from BrüRm@BAR, who died at too young an age.

I have to confess that I am not a fan of any fruit beers, and have not done much experimentation myself in this area. The only advice I can give from tasting such beers is that fresh fruit is the way to go, and fruit syrups or extracts never seem to work well in any beer. There are some examples out there, such as the Fall Line Imperial Stout from Two Beers Brewing in Seattle, Washington, which is aged with cocoa nibs, vanilla bean, and cherries; and I have already mentioned Widmer Brothers' Raspberry Imperial Stout (9.2% abv); also see Cigar City's

Nielsbohrium a little later in this section. Just now, I am drinking a Southern Tier (Lakewood, New York) offering—Plum Noir Imperial Porter (8% abv), which is made with pureed Italian plums. I find it to be a nice, not too sweet Imperial stout, but with no obvious plum flavor. That does not mean that the plums do not contribute any flavor; more likely it means that the brewers have done a good job of ensuring that the beer is well-balanced.

An unusual beer I have come across recently that sort of fits this category is Saranac Caramel Porter (5.4% abv). It is brewed by the long-established Matt Brewing Co. (Utica, New York), which is in its third century of brewing. It claims to use dark caramel malt, Fuggles, and Goldings, along with "caramel color." I don't know what this latter is, but there is a product called "porterine" made by D. D. Williamson & Co. Inc.; it is a coloring derived from corn syrup, and specifically designed for use in beer. I mention it here because porterine has some historical significance, in that it has often been used to convert "regular" beer into porter, rather than by properly formulating the porter. As you might expect, the Saranac beer tastes very sweet and is rather disappointing; it is not one of Saranac's best. You can purchase a caramel flavoring extract as a clear liquid, but this is very concentrated and must be handled with care, because you can easily go overboard and swamp all other flavors. And while on this topic, the same manufacturer has a peanut butter extract, which Jeff Browning at BAR used in a 6% abv stout. He used an extract, rather than actual nuts, since this negates the risk of someone with nut allergies having a reaction to the beer. He called the beer Girl Scout Cookie Stout; I told him he was insane, but actually the beer was pretty good—peanut buttery (of course), but rich and malty still, and very satisfying.

Bourbon is a flavor that does have some promise for porters and stouts. Quite a few craft brewers are turning to the barrel aging of various beers, an approach with a long historical pedigree in the case of porters and stouts. And since bourbon barrels are easily obtainable, storage of beer in them has become almost commonplace. The bourbon flavor obtained in this way can be quite strong, even overpoweringly so, but carefully done can add yet another dimension to an Imperial stout.

Finding examples of such beers is not easy, because they are usually done only as specials and often only on draught; perhaps the best way is to keep close tabs on brewpubs in your vicinity. I recently sampled a very interesting beer from Cigar City Brewing in Tampa, Florida. The first thing is that it is called Nielsbohrium, after Niels Bohr, a hero of mine because he was a leading light in the development of quantum theory in the early twentieth century. This 10% abv beer is made by blending two other Imperial stouts (Dirac and Bohr) and aging the blend in a rum barrel with added raisins and cinnamon. I challenge you to decide which category this beer falls into! This is not something which can be done easily by the homebrewer because of the volume of such barrels (bourbon casks are a nominal 53 US gallons). You could always try adding a little bourbon to a finished beer, which is best done by adding a few drops to a glass and assessing the effect before spoiling a whole batch of beer! Or perhaps a better approach would be to soak a

The old Courage Brewery right by Tower Bridge; it is now a block of luxury apartments.

few oak chips in bourbon, allow them to dry, and then add them to the beer and allow it to sit for a few weeks until you are satisfied with the taste. When you are happy, remove the oak chips—do not just leave them there indefinitely! An example of this is the chocolate oak-aged Yeti Imperial Stout from Great Divide that is produced by aging their wonderful Yeti Imperial Stout on oak chips, along with cocoa nibs and spices. I'll talk a little more about oak and barrel aging in chapter 3.

As a footnote, there are at least a couple of examples of beers aged in other types of barrels. Victory Brewing (Downingtown, Pennsvylania) has a version of their Baltic Thunder that has been aged in a red-wine barrel, and so called Red Thunder. And Two Roads' Igor's Dream, which I referred to earlier, was aged in rye whisky barrels to create a link with *kvass*, a Russian specialty beer made from rye bread. Clearly there is room for more experimentation here, and I look forward to sampling beers aged in other spirit or wine barrels. But please do not even expect me to taste a stout aged in an old pickle barrel!

CHAPTER THREE

PORTER AND STOUT RAW MATERIALS

THE REAL REASON I WANTED TO WRITE THIS BOOK WAS THAT there have been huge changes in the number of materials available to us since I wrote my earlier treatise on porter. Instead of just a simple choice between US 6-row pale or British 2-row pale, we now have a range of base barley malts—one homebrewing catalog I'm looking at now lists no less than twenty examples. And the range of specialty malts is also amazing to one who started brewing when there was only one type of either crystal or black malts. There are more hop varieties than you can shake a mashing oar at, not to mention a multitude of yeast strains. Extract brewers too have a great choice open to them, with not only a number of different manufacturers, but also a range of extracts of varying types and colors. Some of them are manufactured with specialty malts, giving the brewer greater flexibility without any loss in simplicity. And, of course, there is an army of extract kits, among them those designed directly to produce porters and stouts. So in this chapter I am going to describe these ingredients and their use in brewing porters and stouts; to keep things simple, malt extract will be dealt with under base malt.

Bar mirror for a now-defunct East London brewer. Alas, poor Taylor, I knew him well, Horatio.

BASE MALTS

Foremost among these are the pale malts, which can come from either 2-row or 6-row barley. Six-row malts are higher in enzyme content than 2-row malts, and also higher in protein. These characteristics make 6-row malt fine for beers with high adjunct (corn, rice, etc.) levels, where the enzymes can convert the non-malt adjuncts and the nitrogen level is diluted. They are not really as suitable for all-malt beers, and craft brewers generally prefer 2-row malts for their stouts and porters. These may be of Northern American or European origin; in the latter case, Britain is the most important source for our purposes, most Continental European malts being intended for lager brewing. Table 3.1 lists some of the more readily available pale malts, along with the slightly higher dried mild ale malts, which are also very useful in stout and porter brewing. In addition, I have included Vienna and Munich malts, since they, despite being slightly more roasted than pale, both share many aspects of the pale malts, as I'll explain later.

You can use 6-row pale if you wish, but it is generally no cheaper than 2-row malts as far as the homebrewer is concerned. Since we are dealing mostly with all-malt beers, the extra diastatic power of 6-row pale offers no advantage. Most craft brewers prefer to stick to 2-row pale malts, which are considered to give a better flavor for ales, stouts, and porters. Indeed, some brewers are of the opinion that since these beers are essentially British in origin, only the well-modified UK pale malts should be used. In particular, Maris Otter ale malt, which is usually produced using traditional floor-malting methods, is often held to be the base malt of choice for these beers. Maris Otter at its best is a fat, plump grain and does give a full, slightly nutty flavor in ales. However, samples I have seen in recent years are not so plump and have given slightly lower yields than indicated above. Frankly, I think that the quality of current US 2-row pale malts is very good, for they are reasonably well-modified. The risk of forming chill hazes due to their slightly higher protein levels is not important with dark beers, and you may expect to brew good stouts and porters using them. But if you prefer

Table 3.1 Base Malt Properties

Malt	Color, °L	Extract % (Coarse Grind) min.*	Extract SG/lb./gallon**	Protein %	Diastatic power °Lintner
US 6-row pale	1.7-2	77	1.037	12.5-15	140-160
US 2-row pale	1.5-2	78-79	1.038	11-12	110-140
UK 2-row pale	2.5-3.5	81-82	1.039-1.040	9-10	65-70
UK Maris Otter pale	3-4	81-82	1.039-1.040	9-10	40-60
UK mild ale	3.5-4.5	81-82	1.039-1.040	10-10.5	45-50
Briess Ashburne® mild ale	5.3	77	1.037	11.7	65
Vienna***	3-5	76-77	1.036-1.037	13	130
Munich****	8-12	76	1.036	11.7	40

*These are average figures and may vary from sample to sample and from year to year.

**These values are the maximum extracts that can be achieved under ideal conditions. Homebrewers will not obtain these yields; 65 percent of them are a slightly conservative practical figure for what you can expect. In other words, the range for 2-row pale malts of 1.038 to 1.040 (9.5 to 10.0°P) above will be 1.025 to 1.026 (6.3 to 6.6°P) in practice, and these are the numbers I shall use in all recipes.

***The numbers quoted are for US Vienna malt from 6-row barley; samples from other areas, such as Belgium, are likely to be lower in diastatic power.

****This is the most common form of Munich malt, but there are other more roasted types, with colors up to 60°L, which give lower extract yields and are lower in diastatic power, so are probably more properly regarded as being caramel malts.

the apparently more traditional approach of using the British versions, that's fine too, and your choice.

Mild ale malts are rather underrated, simply because relatively few craft brewers make a mild ale (sad, but true). In fact, they are very useful in brewing stouts and porters, since they give both a little extra color and rather more fullness of body, as well as a little more toastiness than their pale malt counterparts. I like them a lot in this context, and any one of the UK or US versions is suitable, particularly for porters. In terms of color and body, Vienna malt is somewhat similar in effect to mild ale malt, except that it gives more of a biscuity rather than toasty note. It has enough enzymes to be the sole base malt, but in porters and stouts, I prefer to use it along with pale malt, in up to 50:50 proportions. At this point, I should mention that I have recently seen an Irish stout malt offered by one of my suppliers; I also know that at least one British maltster (Baird) makes a stout malt, but I have not yet seen it on the North American market. These are both low-colored (1–3°L), and high enough in enzymes to be considered as base malts. Beyond that, I cannot say much, as I have not used them, but they could make for an interesting variation on the base malt theme in both porters and stouts.

Munich malt is a little bit of an oddity in that it is not really a base malt, and is not normally used as the main source of extract. But it does contain sufficient enzymes that it can be used along with pale malt in greater proportion than can specialty malts. I like to use up to 20 to 30 percent of the grist as Munich malt in beers where I want a little extra malty character, such as a robust porter, in which I want to balance out the roast flavor of black malt.

MALT EXTRACT

In terms of base malts, we are obviously looking at straight, unhopped extracts. Hopped beer kits and concentrated brewers worts are formulated to produce specific beers; neither the level of hopping, nor the amount of specialty malts, are generally given. Therefore, it is difficult to give precise recommendations for using these to brew porter or stout. That doesn't mean that you cannot use these extracts for that purpose, but you will have to work it out for yourself, or take the recommendation of a fellow brewer or homebrewing supplier. Or, of course, in the case of a kit or wort specifically designed for porter or stout, simply use as directed and make adjustments to the next brew, according to your liking of the first result.

Unhopped extracts come in two forms: syrup (LME) and dried (DME). The former can have slightly different concentrations, so that one pound in one gallon of water will generally give an SG of 1.034 to 1.037 (8.5 to 9.3°P). DME, on the other hand, will yield a gravity of 1.045 (11.2°P) with one pound in one gallon of water. It is generally used as a "top-up" to ensure reaching the desired wort original gravity without having to go through the often-messy procedure of weighing out small quantities of LME.

Achieving the sort of color and flavor you want for porter or stout can be a little bit of a problem with malt extract. There are several ways around this issue, the first being that of steeping specialty malts (such as crystal or black malt) in hot water and adding the extract to your wort. The second is to do a partial mash of grains which still contain starch, such as brown or amber malt, along with one that contains enzymes, such as pale or even Munich malts. This can be done in a fairly coarse manner, compared to that required for a full mash, and the collected wort is used to dissolve the malt extract.

And, of course, you can use a colored extract, such as amber or dark. These are available in both LME and DME forms, although the liquid form is the most common. Amber extracts work well and are often colored due to the use of Munich, and crystal or caramel malts may still need some further coloring (with, say, black malt, by the steeping approach). Dark extracts are perhaps even better, since they are often produced with high-roast malts such as chocolate, black, and even roasted barley. The disadvantage of colored extracts is that you lose some flexibility, as compared to starting with pale extract and steeping or partial mashing. Nevertheless, they are simple to use, and most of them will give good results.

Not all examples will tell you which specialty malts have been used in their production, which can leave you guessing as to what results they will give, so try to look for those that give you detailed information on their composition. Perhaps the most informative is

A typical malt roaster.

Briess, who not only tells you which malts are used in their amber and dark extracts, but also gives the colors of solutions made with varying amounts of each extract (over a range of solutions with gravities from 1.020 to 1.060 (5.1 to 14.7°P). Briess also produces their Maltoferm® 6000 and 6001 (LME and DME, respectively), which are made from 100 percent black malt. These may not be available from your home-brew supplier, but if they are, they are very useful products for brewing porters and stouts, since they permit you to know exactly how much black malt you have in your recipe! The best source of detailed information on malt extracts is at www.brewingtechniques.com, although this site is now somewhat dated.

SPECIALTY MALTS

Let's start with **caramel** and **crystal** malts. These are highly cured malts prepared by roasting green malt, which in effect involves "stewing" the malt in the presence of moisture. This results in complete hydrolysis of the starch, so the product usually has a glassy interior due to the presence of solidified sugar. This is, of course, where the name crystal malt, a British term, originated. However, a degree of caramelization and color formation also occurs, and American maltsters have opted to call these malts caramel malt. In short, crystal and caramel malts are produced in the same way, and for the same degree of color, they are identical in brewing terms. Some caramel malts may be produced by a kilning (as opposed to roasting) process, and will give different flavor effects than roasted products. "Kilned" caramel can be distinguished from "true" caramel in that the interior of the grain will not be glassy throughout, so it can be regarded in a sense as giving a mixture of caramel and high-roast malt flavors to a beer. The comments that follow will refer only to roasted caramel/crystal malts.

The roasting process can be controlled to give a range of colors and levels of caramelization, and these products are usually designated by color (as 10°, 20°, 40°, 60°, 80°, 120°, and 140°L), the level of color corresponding approximately with the intensity of flavor produced in the beer. The flavor of the lighter crystal/caramel malts is sweet caramel in nature, while the darker ones tend to caramel or toffee, and even somewhat roasty in the highest colored versions. The color added to beer by these malts changes not only in intensity, but also in hue, varying from pale brown for lightly roasted crystal malt up to dark red for the most highly roasted versions. Because crystal/caramel malts contain no starch, they can be steeped in hot water to leach out their extract, and so are suited for easy use with extract beers. But some of this extract is actually unfermentable, so these malts will add some body to beer as well as color and other flavors.

These malts do give a fairly high extract of around 70 to 76 percent, corresponding to an SG of 1.033 to 1.037 (8.3 to 9.3°P) for one pound in one gallon of wort. Homebrewers can expect to get 1.022 to 1.024 SG/lb./gallon (5.6 to 6.1°P), assuming 65 percent brew house efficiency. Crystal malts are very popular with English brewers of all sizes, especially for coloring bitter and pale ales. In the latter cases, I think their use is overdone, and that the Brits tend to overlook the possibilities of using other specialty malts, such as Munich, Vienna, Biscuit, and Victory. I am not suggesting, of course, that crystal malts have no place in porters and stouts, for they do indeed, but we should think not only of them when we want to add caramel-type flavors to a beer.

Crystal/caramel malts are particularly suitable for use in sweet stouts, since those up to about 80°L add to the sweetness and luscious flavor desirable in such beers. For the same reason, they can be used in brewing Baltic porters. They can also be used to advantage in brown and robust porters, especially the latter, in order to balance stronger flavors from the roasted malts, which can also make them useful in both dry and oatmeal stouts. They can be made to work well in American stout, preferably along with other specialty malts, to give the beer enough malt body to balance its high hop rates. Some brewers would advocate using as much as 20 percent of the total malt bill as crystal/caramel, but I think 5 to 10 percent is more appropriate, depending upon what other specialty malts are used. Note that caramel/crystal malts should be used with care in Imperial stouts, as these are big beers and a common flaw in them is that of being too sweet because of the difficulty of obtaining good attenuation. So you don't want to make this worse by adding lots of a malt whose virtue is to provide sweetness in the beer!

Special B malt is a Belgian product; it is really a type of crystal malt, but produced in a manner that gives it a very much different flavor from other crystals. It has been roasted to quite a high color (130 to 150°L) and has a strong caramel and raisin flavor, but none of the roasty notes which are often seen from crystal malts of a similar color. Special B gives a relatively low extract yield at 63 percent, equivalent to 1.030 SG/lb./gallon (7.6°P), or 1.020 (5.1°P) at 65 percent efficiency. It confers a nice warm red hue in a brown porter, and the flavor is such that I would consider its use in any porter or stout, including the Imperial types. It can easily be overdone, for it has a strong enough presence to unbalance the lighter porters and stouts, and I would limit its use to no more than 5 percent of the total grist. Like other caramel malts, Special B can be leached with hot water, so it is easily incorporated into extract brewing schedules.

There are two **biscuit malts** that I think are useful in brewing porters and stouts. First comes Briess Victory® Malt, at 28°L and a potential extract of around 71 percent, equating to 1.034 SG/lb./gallon (8.5°P), or 1.022 (5.6°P) at 65 percent yield. The second is De Wolf-Cosyns Belgian Biscuit Malt, at 23 to 26°L and 77 percent potential extract, or 1.037 SG/lb./gallon (9.3°P), or 1.024 (6.1°P). Both malts, you will be surprised to find, will add biscuit notes to the beer, although they are not identical, as the extract figures will indicate. I find these malts particularly suitable for porters, especially the robust type, but they will also add a nice touch to sweet stouts and help to reduce the one-dimensional character of Irish dry stouts. However, the flavor from them tends to get lost in the bigger Imperial stouts. You can add either of them at the rate of up to 15 percent of the grist, though I generally prefer 5 to 10 percent, depending upon what other specialty malts are in the recipe in question. For extract brewing, these malts are probably best used with the partial mash approach, along with some pale malt.

Special roast malt is a Briess product and weighs in at 63°L, 70 percent extract, 1.033 SG/lb./gallon (8.4°P), 65% of which is about 1.022 SG/lb./gallon (5.6°P). It is quite a complex malt, with its principal flavor contribution being of a bready nature (Briess likens it to a sourdough flavor). It is also dark enough to add a reddish hue to the lighter of the two porters. Special roast adds depth not only to these, but also to both Irish dry and American stouts, nicely rounding off the edges of the latter. I also think it works very well in oatmeal stout, with its bready flavor nicely matching the silkiness of the oat malt. Again, you do not want to overdo it, about 5 percent of the grist is usually sufficient. In an extract brew, I prefer to use this by the partial mash approach, together with an equivalent amount of pale malt.

Melanoidin malt, a Weyermann product, has some similarity to higher dried Munich malts, but is definitely more aromatic and provides a malty fullness in the beer. It has a moderate color at 23 to 31°L, but with somewhat of a reddish hue. It is quite high in extract, with a potential of 76 to 79 percent, 1.036 to 1.038 SG/lb./gallon (9.0 to 9.5°P), or 1.023 to 1.025 SG/lb./gallon (5.8 to 6.3°P) at 65 percent efficiency. It is a malt that is really designed for use in lagers, so that they mimic those produced by decoction mashing. I think it gives pleasing results in oatmeal stout, as well as in Irish dry and American stouts, as it helps to soften the roasted aspects of these beers. It can be added at rates of up to 20 percent of the grist, but I prefer to limit it to about 10 percent, especially when significant amounts of other specialty malts are used. Again, using it in an extract brew would require a partial mash with pale malt to be carried out.

Amber malt is drum-dried, but not really roasted, for it is subjected to a temperature only somewhat slightly higher than would be the case for pale malt. It is modest in color at 20 to 30°L, but still quite high in extract at 70 to 72 percent potential. That is 1.033 to 1.035 SG/lb./gallon (8.3 to 8.8°P), or for our 65 percent target, 1.022 to 1.023 SG/lb./gallon (5.6 to 5.8°P). Amber malt imparts little in the way of sweetness, but does add some body and a biscuity, nutty flavor to porter. In its original form, it was a classical porter ingredient in the late eighteenth and early nineteenth centuries, when many porter grist formulations consisted of 1:1:1 ratio of pale:amber:brown. Modern amber may well be different in flavor to the earlier type, but can still add some complexity, particularly in a brown porter. In my "historical" experiments in porter brewing, I have made several such beers using only brown and pale malt, and these have sometimes been disappointingly one-dimensional. Repeating them with the addition of a proportion of amber yielded much-improved results. Adding it at the rate of 10 to 15 percent of the grist is usually the best way to go for a straightforward brown porter. You can use it at higher rates if you wish, with little effect on color, but I find its flavor somewhat subtle, so that it is best used in smaller amounts along with other specialty malts. Because of its subtlety, it does come off well in a sweet stout, adding some depth and taking the edge off the sweetness. For the same reason, I might not use it in a dry or American stout, where it would be overwhelmed by the roast character of black malt. On the other hand, it is well worth thinking of adding some to your Baltic porter recipe, since that style of beer is so often dominated by sweetness. In the case of Imperial stout, it can be a part of the cast of specialty malts added to give the beer complexity. Just remember that in such big beers (± 10% abv), where the total amount of malt is high, an addition rate of 5 percent of the total represents a higher actual weight of malt than it would in a brown porter at a much lower original gravity.

Amber malt does contain some starch and must be used in a partial mash along with some pale malt if you want to use it in an extract-based brew. However, since you probably do not wish to make your partial mash too big in volume, you may want to use it in only small amounts, along with the more flavorful brown or biscuit malts. And by the way, it is a malt that is fairly easy to make at home, and I have done so.

In historical terms, **brown malt** is *the* porter malt, for it was quoted as being the sole malt used in porter brewing. It was sometimes called "blown" or high-dried malt, because the kiln heat was raised very quickly after the first stage of drying, which would cause the grain to "pop." This resulted in a product that apparently still contained enough in the way of starch-converting enzymes to permit obtaining fermentable extract from the malt by the usual mashing process. I still have trouble seeing how that could be the case; maybe I'll work it out one day? Anyway, this is perhaps academic, since modern brown malt is drum-dried and contains no enzymes to break down its residual starch. Does it in any way match the flavor of the original? At one time, my answer would have been probably not, because it was generally held that brown malt was not being made after the First World War, a casualty of war-time restrictions on roasting malt. Well, thanks to my own research with the specialist maltsters French and Jupp, and those of Ron Pattinson (*Pattinson,* 2010) into the brewing books of various London brewers, it is clear that brown malt has remained in production right up to the present day. Then, since there has been no break in making it, could it be that there has not been a great flavor change in this malt, even though the manufacturing process has changed somewhat? After all, when the change was made from kiln- to drum-drying, would not the maltster have tried to at least more or less match the older product? Well, that's my "thought experiment" on it; one of much less significance than any of Einstein's thought experiments, and one with much less chance of ever being proven correct.

Modern brown malt is dried to a higher temperature than is amber malt, making it darker in color (50 to 70°L), with an extract potential of around 71 percent (but see below). So we are looking at 1.034

SG/lb./gallon (8.5°P), or 1.022 SG/lb./gallon (5.6°P) for 65 percent efficiency. As a specialty malt, brown has almost everything—it will add some sweetness, some biscuity (graham cracker?) character, some toasted notes, caramel, toffee, and licorice. I advise you not to try using it on its own, like the original, because it contains enough starch to cause a really sticky set mash. It can only be used when mashed along with pale malt. I've found that you can go as high as a 50:50 mix of US 2-row pale and brown, and still get good extraction, with no risk of a set mash. That is probably higher than you want to go in most cases, and about 20 percent of the grist would be a good top limit for most brews.

Now, what I have described is brown malt from the UK. Just recently, Briess has released its Carabrown® Malt, which they quote as being on the light side of the brown malt style. It typically has a color at 55°L, and Briess quotes an extract of 79 percent on a fine grind basis. The latter is really only attainable in the laboratory, and we are more concerned with the corresponding coarse grind extract, as are all the other values I have given in this section. The latter is normally a lower figure, by about 2 to 3 percent, so I estimate we're looking at 76 percent extract for this malt. That would put the yield close to 1.036 SG/lb./gallon (9.1°P), so at 65 percent efficiency, we get 1.023 SG/lb./gallon (5.8°P). I have brewed two identical porters, one of them using UK brown malt and the other using Briess Carabrown®; there was some difference in color and wort gravity, but that was marginal in the context of the recipe I used. More importantly, I could not observe any significant differences in flavor in the finished beers, except that the one using UK brown might have been just a touch drier and toastier, and the one using Briess malt was perhaps a shade nuttier in the middle of the palate.

So, essentially, either of amber or brown malts would serve well in a porter. In fact, I think that brown malt is just about a "must" for both styles of porter, and for all our stout types. Obviously I like brown malt a lot, as you will have deduced from the length of this sub-section, and would use it at the rate of anywhere from 5 to 20 percent of the grist in all my beers in these categories. There is no question that it confers unique flavor characteristics on any such beer. Perhaps the only caveat I have is that if you use a grist consisting of only pale and brown malts, the resulting beer can be a little disappointing, and almost flat in flavor.

But in combination with one or more other specialty malts, such as Special B, caramel, or roasted malts like chocolate or black, you will find your porters and stouts have moved to a whole new dimension.

It will be obvious from the above that you will need to do a partial mash with this malt and some pale malt, along with the specialty malts of your choice, in your extract brewing. If you have not yet tried partial mashing, the improvement this malt can give you makes it well worth the effort, so give it a try!

Chocolate malt is a high-roast product whose name really refers to its color, but it does add a chocolate-like flavor to beer. Yet the color of chocolate malt covers quite a range and varies from one manufacturer to another. Table 3.2 lists the products from some well-known manufacturers:

Table 3.2 Available Chocolate Malts

Designation	Manufacturer*	Color °L	Extract %
chocolate	Briess	350	71**
2-row chocolate	Briess	350	73**
dark chocolate	Briess	420	70**
pale chocolate	Thomas Fawcett	185–250	71
chocolate	Thomas Fawcett	325–400	71
chocolate	Franco-Belges	300–375	
chocolate	Crisp	425–475	75**
chocolate	Baird	450–500	72
chocolate	Muntons	340–420	71
chocolate	Simpson	375–450	73
chocolate	Dingemans	300–380	
chocolate	Pauls	415–490	73
CARAFA® I	Weyermann	300–375	
CARAFA® II	Weyermann	413–450	
CARAFA® III	Weyermann	480–563	

*Figures are from respective companies' websites
**Estimate from fine grind figure

The point I want to make about the different color levels is that the higher the color, the more highly the malt has been roasted. Therefore, the higher the color, the stronger the flavor effect will be for a given rate of addition. Indeed, at the very top of the color spectrum given above, this malt comes close to the color of black malt, so that the flavor can be expected to be somewhat harsh, with less cocoa-type or nutty flavor. In other words, if you are making a brown porter, you might want to use chocolate malt with a color below 400°L at a rate of no more than 5 percent of the grist, or even Fawcett's pale chocolate at up to 10 percent of the grist. On the other hand, if you are brewing an American stout and you want some roast character to balance the hoppiness, but don't want the harsher flavor from black malt, you would probably go with 5 to 10 percent of one of the chocolate malts above 400°L.

Basically, chocolate malt is suited to any porter or stout, at a rate of 10 percent of the grist at a maximum. In choosing which one, you should first define what you are trying to do with that particular beer (which you really ought to be doing in any case) before you select the malt bill. That will decide what other specialty malts you might want to add; since you do not normally want to add above 20 percent of the base malt in total, this choice will limit how much chocolate malt you can add. In Irish dry stout (or foreign extra stout, where black is the dominant roasted malt), you may still wish to include a little chocolate (up to 5 percent) to ensure that the beer is not too harsh. If you want to use a lot of brown malt (15 to 20 percent), then you might eliminate chocolate, since its flavor notes can be swamped by those from the brown. But in the case of an Imperial stout, you may add it simply because you are throwing in some of just about every other specialty malt to give the beer more complexity, so that its underlying sweetness is muted.

Chocolate malt gives a fair proportion of extract, despite being high-roasted, with 71 percent being about average. This represents 1.034 SG/lb./gallon (8.5°P), or at 65 percent efficiency, 1.022 SG/lb./gallon (5.6°P). All of this (including the flavor components) is leached out by steeping in hot water, so that chocolate malt is ideal for use in extract brewing of porter and stouts.

Note that Weyermann also has its CARAFA® Special I, II, and III, which match those in Table 3.2 for color, but are made from dehusked barley. They should give a similar level of extract, but a somewhat smoother flavor than other chocolate malts, although I do not necessarily consider their use an advantage in porters and stouts. Weyermann goes even further and offers chocolate wheat malt (300 to 450°L) and chocolate rye malt (188 to 300°L), both of which offer some subtle variations, especially in brown porter and sweet stout.

Black malt was invented in the early nineteenth century by Daniel Wheeler, who patented his invention, and it is still sometimes called "patent malt," or "patent black malt," even though that patent has long since expired. It was the first high-roast malt to be produced, and was quickly incorporated into beers by the porter manufacturers. It is also the highest roasted malt available, since taking the roasting any higher would simply result in charring the malt to carbon. In fact, until relatively recently, charring and even ignition of the malt in the process was such a risk

A memorial to a malt kiln destroyed by a fire at French & Jupp.

that a man would stand by with a pail of water to douse the malt and prevent a fire if the roasting got out of hand!

Table 3.3 Details of Black Malt Varieties

Manufacturer*	Designation	Color °L	Extract %
Baird	black malt	500–600	68
Crisp	black malt	580–630	73
Thomas Fawcett	black malt	410–500	71
Simpsons	black malt	500–600	73
Briess	black malt	500	68**
Briess	2-row black malt	500	69**
Briess	Black Prinz®***	500	
Briess	Midnight Wheat	550	
Briess	black malted barley flour	500	
Castle Malt	de-bittered black***	500–600	63
Franco-Belges	Kiln black	450–585	
Dingemans	de-bittered black malt***	500–600	
Paul's	black	510–585	71**
Muntons	black	416–490	70

*Figures are from respective companies' websites
**Estimate from fine grind figure
***All these malts are made from de-husked barley

Despite this, black malt does come in somewhat different levels of color according to who produces it, as can be seen in Table 3.3.

Clearly there is some variation in the color of these products, although the color they produce in beer is so intense that these differences are hardly significant, at least to the naked eye. It is of course a black color, which many people see as the main characteristic of stout, and to a lesser extent of robust porter. The principal flavor conferred on beer by black malt is that of highly roasted coffee, but with an underlying acrid harshness and astringency, the latter of which can dominate if the addition rate is too high. And remember that you do not need to get all the color from black malt, since other roasted malts, such as chocolate and brown, contribute dark colors without adding harshness. Indeed, I would almost always think of using a combination of these three malts in stout brewing, rather than using black malt alone. But black malt is almost mandated as an ingredient for robust porter and all stouts.

In Table 3.3, I have listed three de-bittered black malts, along with Briess's Midnight Wheat, which they describe as "bitterless." These are all designed to give color and a smooth, roasted chocolate/coffee flavor with no harsh astringent taste. But they are really intended merely for coloring beers other than stouts (such as black IPA or Schwarzbier), and offer much less in the way of the roast character than do regular black malts. Therefore, I think their use in brewing stouts and porters is somewhat limited except in special cases, such as if you are looking for a slightly darker color in a brown porter without upsetting its balance. However, I have included them here (and given one or two recipes incorporating them) so that you are aware of them, and can experiment with them if you so wish.

There is some variation in the extract potential of these malts, as you can see from the table. However, the average of the values in the table is 70 percent, so that you can expect 1.033 SG/lb./gallon (8.4°P), 65 percent of which is 1.021 SG/lb./gallon (5.3°P). Black malt can, and perhaps should be used in robust porters and in all forms of stout (although note that Baltic porter is perhaps better colored with a de-bittered black malt). Addition rates can obviously vary, but in general 1 to 5 percent of grist is as much as you need. Many stouts are brewed with roasted barley as well as black malt, and I would recommend you keep the combination of these to a maximum of 5 percent of the total, or these two malts can make your beer very one-dimensional, with the roast flavors obliterating all others.

How you add black malt is a matter for some debate. Since both extract and color are readily leached out with hot water, malt extract brewers can obviously do a steep of it (along with any other non-starchy specialty malts) or include it in a partial mash, if you want to use a starch-containing malt such as amber or brown. But for all-grain brewers, there are other options available. The obvious approach is to add it directly to the mash, and many home and craft brewers do exactly that. But some believe that this will result in extracting more of the harsh flavor from this malt than they want, and try to avoid it. In the mid-nineteenth century, Northgate Brewery in Bath, England, just like a malt extract brewer, actually steeped black malt with hot water in a vessel kept just for that purpose. The liquor from the steep was run off the malt and added directly to the wort boil.

Another approach is to use Briess's Black Malt Flour (see Table 3.3), which is a very fine, powdery product that has a high surface area per unit weight, which permits rapid extraction of flavor and color on contact with a hot liquid. It can be added directly to the boiling wort, or as we have done at BrüRm@BAR, to the wort at knockout. Of course, we have an efficient whirlpool, so most of the malt flour remains with the trub. What does not settle out in this way will be entrapped by the yeast at the end of fermentation. And if any of it should pass through with the beer, it will be taken out when it is filtered before transfer to the serving tank. Our results were certainly satisfactory, although I must admit we did not do a control test! Homebrewers who want to use this flour should be careful in their trub and yeast separations, so as to make sure none of the flour goes through into the finished beer. If it does so, at best it will mean that the beer is difficult to clear, and at worst you will actually ingest some of it when you drink the beer, which will accentuate the astringency you have been trying to avoid!

Those of you who are still awake will see immediately that **roasted barley** is not really a malt at all, since it is the raw grain that has been roasted. However, since it is very often used alongside black malt in stouts, I have included it here; besides, some English authorities have designated it as being a "special malt." I am not sure who first came up with this idea, but it seems that it might have been Guinness, who originally did it purely as an economic measure, since roasted barley was cheaper than black malt, which had to go through an expensive malting process before being roasted. Indeed, the barley used for this does not even need to be of malting quality, which makes it cheaper still. Regardless, its use became a signature note in Irish dry stouts and foreign extra stout, and it is also frequently used in all other stouts: sweet, oatmeal, American, and Imperial. It can also be used in small

Table 3.4 Roasted Barley Types			
Maltster[*]	Designation	Color °L	Extract %
Baird	Roasted Barley	500–600	68
Crisp	Roasted Barley	500–560	77
Simpson	Roasted Barley	500–600	73
Munton	Roasted Barley	500–600	74
Fawcett	Roasted Barley	410–500	70
Briess	Roasted Barley	300	70[**]
Briess	Black Barley	500	68[**]

[*]Figures are from respective companies' websites
[**]Estimated from fine grind figures

amounts in robust porter, but should be avoided in brown and Baltic porters. In the case of Irish dry stout, it is often used along with both black malt and flaked barley in order to simulate Guinness Extra Stout.

There is some variation in both color and potential extract with roast barleys, so Table 3.4 lists the details for the major maltsters.

It is plain that there is quite a range of colors and extracts, although the latter is not too important in the context of the grain being used in only small proportions. But it is likely that there is some difference in flavor between the various products, since the lighter the color, the less strong the sharp and acrid flavor will be. For most of the products above, that difference will not be significant if the addition rate is kept at 1 to 5 percent. However, it will be different for Briess Roasted Barley, which should give a smoother, less sharp or harsh flavor and could potentially be used in slightly higher proportions. However, there probably will not be many instances where you might want to use more of this grain. It might be advantageous to use a little roasted barley in a beer where you would not otherwise normally use it, such as a Baltic porter, and in that case, you might as well go for the Briess product. But in general, you will be using roasted barley because you want to have some of that roast flavor in the beer, such as in an Imperial stout or Irish dry stout, and nothing else will do.

Roasted barley is not identical to black malt, and tends to give a drier, even grainier finish to the beer. That is why a combination of the two is so effective in an Irish dry stout. Average extract from the table is 71 percent, or 1.034 SG/lb./gallon (8.5°P), 65 percent of which is 1.022 SG/lb./gallon (5.6°P). This extract can be virtually entirely leached out with hot water, so is easily incorporated into a malt extract-based brew.

Like roasted barley, **flaked barley** is not, of course, a malted grain. Indeed, it is generally used purely as an adjunct, or malt substitute. I include it here simply because I do not intend to include a separate section on adjuncts, and because it is often used alongside roasted barley in Irish dry stout, usually in the belief that the beer so brewed will match Guinness Extra Stout. It is best used in its pre-gelatinized form, and needs to be added to an all-grain mash (bad news for malt extract brewers!). It is low in color (1 to 1.5°L), and gives about 68 percent potential extract, or 1.033 SG/lb./gallon, or 1.022 SG/lb./gallon (5.6°P) at 65 percent efficiency. It can be added at rates of 10 to 15 percent of the grist, and its effect on flavor is minimal, except to make the beer slightly drier. Flaked barley is also thought to improve head retention, so is useful in a beer where you want a fine dense head, which Guinness Extra Stout is famous for. That's the theory, but I think it is more often used by commercial brewers simply to reduce raw material costs. In any case, we are concerned here with all-malt beers, where head retention is unlikely to be a problem. So the good news for extract brewers is that you don't really need to bother with using this adjunct; if you feel you must do so, then it will need to be incorporated into a partial mash.

For oatmeal stouts, there are both **oat malt** and **oat flakes** to consider. Fawcett offers an oat malt at 2 to 4°L, and 70 percent extract—1.033 SG/lb./gallon (8.4°P), 1.022 SG/lb./gallon (5.6°P) at 65 percent efficiency. Simpson, on the other hand, produces Golden Naked Oats at a somewhat higher color of 6 to 14°L, with 73 percent extract or 1.035 /lb./gallon (8.8°P), 65 percent of which is 1.023 SG/lb./gallon (5.8°P). In the United States, Briess makes oat flakes at 2.5°L, and 70 percent extract and 1.033 SG/lb./gallon (8.4°P), or 1.022 SG/

lb./gallon (5.6°P) at 65 percent yield. Any of these can be used in brewing oatmeal stout, for I have found no real difference between them in an otherwise quite strongly flavored beer, although Simpson claims that its product has "a special, sweet berry-nut flavor." That may be so, but such a flavor may be lost in an oatmeal stout, where the main purpose of oat malt/oat flakes is to confer a smooth silkiness to the beer's palate. It is a flavor effect much prized by many drinkers, although I find it somewhat elusive.

The use of oat malt/oat flakes is recommended by suppliers at the rate of 5 to 25 percent of the grist in oatmeal stout. I do not like to go above 10 percent, because oats can cause a problem with the mash, making it sticky and wort run-off slow, so it is best not to use too much, in my view. These oat products must be mashed, so that extract brewers can only use them via a partial mash, in which case you must be careful to use significantly more pale malt (about two times as much) than oat malt or oat flakes to minimize any "sticky" problems.

Rye malt is also worth considering in the context of stout brewing, and it is produced by both Weyermann and Briess in the United States. In terms of color (3 to 5°L) and extract (generally around 75 percent, but I have seen it quoted as high as 84 percent), it might seem that rye malt should be considered along with the base malts. I have included it here because I consider it a "flavor adjuster" in this context. In other words, it is a malt to be used as only a small part of the grist so as to add a little extra flavor and complexity to the beer. It is also a malt that should not be used in large proportions (greater than 20 percent of the total) because it can result in a very sticky mash with low wort run-off rates. Rye malt tends to give the beer a drier flavor, with a characteristic spicy note that goes well in Imperial, oatmeal, and sweet stouts, when added at the rate of 5 to 10 percent of the grist. Small amounts (2 to 5 percent) can be added to brown and robust porters for a little more depth in the malt palate, as well as American stouts, where it can help to balance the high hop flavors. I do not like it in Irish dry or foreign extra stout, because it only helps to make them drier and accentuate the malt acidity. It can also add a slight reddish hue to beer, so that, with its spicy character, makes it a good option for adding around

10 percent of the grist for a Baltic porter, a beer that really needs all the complexity it can get!

At 75 percent extract, we are looking at 1.036 SG/lb./gallon (9.1°P), so 65 percent efficiency will give us 1.023 SG/lb./gallon (5.8°P). Rye malt needs to be mashed, but even though it has sufficient enzymes for full starch conversion, mashing it on its own is going to produce a sticky mess. Therefore, extract brewers would have to use it in a partial mash at the rate of 20:80 of rye to pale malt as a maximum.

There is an alternative approach for extract brewers who want to get some of that rye flavor into their beer, and that is to use caramel/crystal rye malt. Weyermann offers CARARYE®, a caramel rye malt at 57 to 76°L, which should give around 70 percent extract, 1.033 SG/lb./gallon (8.3°P), or 1.022 (5.6°P) at 65 percent. This can be used to give a reddish hue and the typical spicy rye flavor at up to 15 percent of the grist. Both Thomas Fawcett and Baird produce crystal rye malts that are slightly darker than the one above, at 70 to 80°L and 80 to 100°L. Potential extracts are pretty much as with the caramel rye malt, which are recommended to be used at up to 5 percent of the grist. The great advantage of these in extract brewing is that they do not require mashing, but can simply be steeped in hot water, as with the other caramel/crystal malts, without the need to do a partial mash and without the risk of getting a sticky mess, as with standard rye malt.

For the record, Weyermann also makes Chocolate Rye malt, roasted to the relatively low color (for a chocolate malt, that is) of 190 to 300°L, which can be expected to give a similar extract to those of other chocolate malts. It is claimed to give an enhanced aroma to beer, as well as adding color. I haven't tried it, so I am not sure whether it would provide much in the way of the typical flavor associated with rye malts.

Smoked malts must be thought of as a potential ingredient for porters and stouts. As I have already pointed out, the original eighteenth-century porters might well have had a smoky flavor, so if you want to be truly traditional, or if you just like the flavor of smoke, you may want to incorporate smoked malt into your porter. In general, it is mainly porters that are considered in this context, for I can't recall seeing any smoked stouts about. But there is no reason why they should not exist, nor any reason why you should not make a smoked-Russian-oatmeal-Imperial-milk stout, if that is what fulfills your desire for experimentation!

There are at least five commercially available smoked malts, three wood-smoked and two peat-smoked. They are all pale in color (2 to 4°L), and high in extract potential (78 to 81 percent), or 1.037 to 1.039 SG/lb./gallon (9.3 to 9.8°P). With only a 65 percent yield, that translates to 1.024 to 1.025 SG/lb./gallon (6.1 to 6.3°P). These malts should not be considered to be identical in terms of the quality of smoke flavor they will add to a beer. Weyermann's Smoked and Best Malz Smoked are German rauch malts, while the Briess version is smoked over cherrywood. Weyermann and Best Malz state that their products can be used at rates of up to 100 percent of the grist, whilst Briess indicates that theirs gives an intense smoke flavor and should not be used at more than 60 percent, and suggests a rate of 30 to 60 percent for stouts and porters. That seems rather high to me, because I find that the smoke flavor can easily overpower all others, and I would go for 10 to 20 percent of the grist in a brown or robust porter. Perhaps you could use more of this malt in a big Imperial stout, depending upon your personal preference. As a reference point, I should say that the smoke flavor in a Bamberg Rauch Bier is just too much for me to be able to take more than a few sips of it! The way to go about it is to use a modest amount the first time you try a particular recipe, make careful note of the beer's flavor, and adjust the addition rate up or down on the repeat brew, as your palate dictates.

Simpson and Thomas Fawcett both offer peated malts, which are very different from the other two, with somewhat more of a phenolic character in the smoke flavor conferred on beer. The analyses cited indicate that Simpson's version may be the smokier of the two, for what that is worth. Extract yields and color are much the same as the wood-smoked malts above. Their use is recommended at a rate of no more than 1 to 10 percent of the grist, and I would go for a maximum of 5 percent. It is not really related to the original porter malts, since these were generally dried over woods such as beech and hornbeam, although some of the early ones were even dried with straw. Nevertheless, peated malt can add a unique quality to your beer, so if you are looking for an extra bit of complexity, it is worth considering.

Because it requires only relatively small amounts of peated malt, and because it contains starch-degrading enzymes, this malt is easy to use in brewing an extract beer. You would need to do a partial mash with about half to one pound of peated malt, plus any other specialty malts you plan to use which require mashing. The wood-smoked malts might also be used alone in a partial mash, say up to about two pounds for a five-gallon brew. See my comments on addition rates above, and remember the dictum "Brew one, try one, brew another one."

A final point about smoked malts is that I have often found them to be somewhat variable in their flavor effect. I suspect that this is the result of the conditions of storage, so that for reproducible results, you should try to use as fresh a sample as you can obtain. Don't buy more than you need for the beer you are currently brewing, and do not leave any unused amounts in the back of your grain storage space for a year or two before using it! Or you can take another route, and smoke your own malt and use it right away. That, of course, leaves room for quite a bit of experimentation in smoking techniques, types of wood, and so on, making for a topic of discussion that is beyond the scope of this book.

As I write this, it occurred to me that **acidulated malt** might offer a relatively easy way to get a sour edge into Irish dry stout and foreign extra stout. I have already remarked that these beers, as brewed by Guinness, did have such a flavor, as probably did the original porters. Acidulated malt could be added in relatively small proportion so that its lactic acid content would give some sourness to your beer. Such malt is produced by the action of lactic acid–producing bacteria on "normal" grain, and is designed for adjustment of mash pH for brewing in accordance with the Reinheitsgebot. Both Weyermann and Best Malz produce acidulated malt at 1.8°L, and extract at around 77 percent, which equates to 1.037 SG/lb./gallon (9.3°P), or at 65 percent efficiency 1.024 SG/lb./gallon (6.1°P). And Weyermann actually offers a malt bill for "Berliner Weisse" that includes 8 percent acidulated malt to give the beer its characteristic sour taste. So addition at a slightly lower rate, say up to 5 percent, might just work well for your Irish dry and foreign stout.

However, be aware that although the original porters and probably Guinness Foreign Stout did almost certainly contain significant levels of lactic acid, there were probably other flavor-producing organisms present, such as *Brettanomyces* yeast species. So you might want to try incorporating a *Brettanomyces* species of yeast into your fermentation if you are really trying to re-create old porters and stouts. That is relatively complicated to do, because of the slow rate of *Brettanomyces* fermentations and the difficulty of controlling them. That is why I have suggested that you might want to consider using acidulated malt, because it is simple to incorporate it in your mash (or partial mash

An ad for Hull's Porter, demonstrating that they were still brewing porter in the 1950s.

extract beer), and because it will give you a fairly precise level of lactic acid in the beer, as the malt no longer contains acid-producing bacteria. Or, of course, you may just decide that you do not want to try to match the Guinness flavor or any eighteenth-century porter, and that you do not want a sour edge in your beer at all!

FLAVORINGS

I never intended to go into the use of various flavorings in porter and stout brewing, partly because it is a limitless area, and partly because it is a very subjective matter as to what flavor you want and at what level you want it in your beer. However, there are now so many such flavored beers available, I have to make at least a few comments in this area. Now, there are a variety of synthetic flavorings on the market (including porterine), which come as liquids, are food-safe, and easy to add to beer (see, for example, www.capellaflavors.com). I do not intend to say anything more about them, as I have no experience using them, and I tend to take the more traditional view that you can achieve such a range of flavors using the malts and hops available to us that I don't want to bother with synthetic additives. But you should be aware that they are out there, and there's nothing to stop you from playing about with them in your porters and stouts. If you do so, be careful, because they are often very intensely flavored, and you should always do a small scale test on a pint or so of beer before adding anything to the bulk.

Next on this list has to be **lactose**, if only because I haven't mentioned it elsewhere in this chapter, although I did discuss it under sweet stout in chapter 2. Indeed, sweet stout is its only application in this field. In order to avoid repetition, I shall just say here that it is a sugar which is unfermentable by brewing yeasts. It therefore adds only sweetness, though only about 40 percent of the sweetness of a similar concentration of sucrose. Since it is normally dissolved in the wort near the end of the boil, it serves well in either extract or all-grain brewing. It is commonly added at around 2 to 3 percent by weight of the total grist, or about one pound in five US gallons (19L). At this addition rate, it will add about SG 1.012 to both your original and finishing gravities.

Licorice is a root that may not have been the first thing to come to mind under flavorings, but in fact has a long history of use in porters. Around the end of the eighteenth and early nineteenth centuries, many publicans and brewers in England were looking for substitutes for brown malt, and licorice was one of them. In fact, it was one of the few such additives used at the time that was not toxic in one way or another, and it is still appropriate to use it in porter brewing, and even in stouts if you like. It is available from homebrew suppliers as a 5-inch stick weighing just under an ounce (25g, to be exact), and can be added during the last half hour or so of the wort boil. It will give the beer a pleasant anise or licorice flavor (surprise, surprise), somewhat similar to that from brown malt. That makes it a good candidate for an extract-based porter, where you do not want to bother with brown malt and a partial mash, but do want to get some of that malt's flavor in the beer.

Vanilla is an additive with a flavor that goes well in a brown porter, since it adds a nice clean, just slightly spicy touch to this well-balanced beer. It does not take much; just add anywhere between a half to two vanilla beans in a five-gallon brew, according to your taste (I've seen one recipe recommending up to five beans, but that seems to be over the top). But where to add it is the question, and as with the other flavorings discussed in this section, everybody seems to have a different answer to the question. Some add it in the boil, some at the end of the boil, some at the end of fermentation, while yet another recommends extracting the beans with vodka for a week, and adding the alcoholic extract in the secondary.

It seems to me that the vodka extraction approach might be the most efficient, since this is the way that pure vanilla extract is made. The latter is obviously available, although said to be quite expensive, but would be easy to use. Just take a pint glass of the beer after fermentation and add the extract drop by drop (be sure to keep count) until you get the flavor you want. Multiply it up and add to the bulk of the beer at bottling or kegging. This is obviously a method very well-adapted to extract as well as all-grain brewing.

A cheaper approach is to buy vanilla flavoring, which is also alcohol-based; it is made by mixing artificial vanillin with sugar and other flavorings. According to one source, this works almost as well as the pure extract, so it might be worth using this in your first "vanilla brew," so as to get a feel for the effect before trying one of the more expensive approaches with the pure extract of the bean itself.

I have had more than a few good **coffee**-flavored stouts, and brewed one or two on a commercial scale. I think the approach is first to use a tried and tested stout/porter recipe, one that you have enjoyed on its own. Then brew it again, but this time add your coffee, which brings us to the questions of which coffee to use, and where and how it should be incorporated in the brewing process. After all, there are an awful lot of coffees out there, and quite a few different ways of preparing them. In fact, there are so many that I shall not even attempt to recommend particular types, although I'll give an example below. In selecting one (or a mixture), you have to think about what you want to achieve with this beer. Is your aim primarily to improve the beer's aroma, or do you simply want to add that good roasty flavor into the mix of the beer's palate? Is the beer big enough to stand up to your planned treatment? Buckets of espresso coffee added to a modest brown porter would probably result in the production of an alcoholic coffee rather than a beer, while two teaspoons of a mild roast won't be noticeable in an Imperial stout!

The choice of coffee also depends on how you are going to add it during brewing. You are likely going to get the most flavor and aroma out of the coffee by a hot, rather than a cold, extraction. You can add it to the hot wort, but not during or after fermentation, unless you pre-brew the coffee in the normal manner. Many craft brewers consider this latter approach to be the best way to obtain the rich aroma they want in their beer. And it has the advantage that you do not have to worry about removing coffee grounds from the beer at any stage. Certainly, adding pre-prepared coffee after fermentation is a great way to determine how much to add. Just go through the routine I described above with vanilla by treating a sample of the beer with the coffee until you are satisfied, then scale up to the whole batch.

Of course there are always contrarians, which in this case are those who think they can get the flavor and aroma they want by adding the ground beans to hot wort. This is usually done either five to ten minutes before the end of the boil, or at the end of the boil and allowing them to steep for a few minutes before the wort is cooled. If you do this, you may find it advantageous to use a steeping bag, such as the muslin bags often used for dry hopping, so that the coffee grounds can be easily removed and will not cause subsequent clogging of things like coolers or siphon tubes. Of course, whichever route you choose, you should always go with freshly ground coffee, and not something that has sat in a jar or can for weeks.

At BrüRm@BAR, we take an even more diverse route in our Espresso Stout. Firstly, the "base" stout is our regular stout, which is really an American stout, but more lightly hopped than is usual for the style. The coffee comes from a specialist supplier and is ground the morning of brew day. We brew 11.5 barrels (356 gallons), and add the coffee thus: two pounds Kenya Roast, two pounds Espresso, and one pound Breakfast Blend to the mash, just before sparging; one pound Kenya Roast, one pound Espresso, and one pound Breakfast Blend at the end of the boil, when we have a ten-minute rest before starting the whirlpool. In the last version, we added two pounds Breakfast Blend and one pound Espresso to the fermenter at the end of the primary fermentation—a variation along the theme of dry-hopping.

It may not be the standard approach, but we like the result, and consider the "dry-bean" version the best we have made, with just the right amount of coffee flavor and aroma without overpowering the beery character of the stout. Although we will probably tweak it one way or another the next time we brew it!

Craft brewers seem to like **chocolate** flavor in stouts, rather than in porters. Not, of course, in Irish dry or foreign extra stout, nor in American stout, where the hop flavors and bitterness would not go well with the taste of chocolate. But when it comes to oatmeal, and particularly Imperial stouts, the addition of a little chocolate richness can produce some very interesting beers. The type of chocolate used is important, and that with a high proportion of cocoa and low cocoa butter content is what you want. It is generally held that cocoa butter, being a fat, will inhibit head retention (although at least one brewer thinks the fat is useful as a yeast nutrient). So look for something with lots of cocoa, including cocoa itself, and no sweeteners or other additives (which are often present in regular "eating" chocolate). Many brewers like to use chocolate nibs (which are essentially raw chocolate taken right after the beans have been roasted, and do actually contain quite a bit of cocoa butter!). You should use a base stout brewed with a goodly proportion of chocolate malt (up to 10 percent of the grist), and will probably need to add three to five ounces (90 to 140g) of cocoa, or cocoa plus unsweetened chocolate in a five-gallon (19L) brew. You may need more or less than that, depending upon the strength of the stout, how much chocolate flavor you want in it, and on how strongly flavored the cocoa/chocolate is. As always, it is better to be a little conservative at first and adjust in the next brew, rather than charging in and producing something barely drinkable.

The best addition point is at the start of the boil, since this reduces the risk of any fat carrying over into fermentation. If you are not happy with the results when it comes to bottling or kegging, you can always adjust the chocolate flavor using a fat-free extract, and adding to taste. These extracts are designed to enhance the flavor of a baking product that already contains chocolate, and are probably not suitable as the primary source of chocolate in stout. But this is a relatively new area for brewers, so there is a lot of room for experimentation, and for new, more suitable products to become available to us. So keep your eyes open for "brewers' chocolate" coming onto the market!

An interesting and still-developing area in brewing is that of introducing **barrel-aged** flavors. For some years now, craft brewers have been interested in barrel-aging in order to get otherwise unobtainable flavors in beer. This is an interesting historical reversal, for in the days when beer was always kept in wooden casks and kegs, brewers mostly tried to prevent the beer from picking up flavor from the wood. Now that draft beer generally comes in stainless steel casks and kegs, some do want to get flavor out of the wood. You don't want to use barrels that have been used for beer over and over again, since the wood flavor compounds will have been completely leached out. Most craft brewers go for barrels that have been used only once, such as wine and spirit barrels. Those used for bourbon aging have become particularly popular, and I have tasted some very interesting beers aged in such barrels. As a matter of fact, Wynkoop brewed a strong ale from a recipe that I found from an Oxford college brewery; it is currently maturing nicely in a used bourbon barrel somewhere in the depths of Wynkoop's cellars, but that's another story.

I have already pointed out that such barrels are not of much use to the homebrewer, simply because of their capacity. You can get smaller barrels, usually new, but the aging effect is quite different, probably because a five-gallon barrel has a much larger surface area per unit of volume than a fifty-gallon barrel. Further, any beer brewed in this way is going to be a one-off, for each barrel will give different results depending upon the original level of charring and on its previous contents. And even if you were to use the same barrel for a second brew, you will get a different beer, because many, if not all of the flavor components, will have been leached out by the first brew. There are ways for homebrewers to simulate barrel-aging, and to do it so that the results are reproducible. I haven't experimented with them much, so I am just going to make a few general points.

In most cases, your stout is going to age on the oak for some time, so it is generally preferable to do it with a big beer (7 percent abv and above), the alcohol in which will help to limit possible bacterial contamination. If you are not going to use an actual barrel, many suppliers offer oak essence and powder, as well as oak chips and oak cubes, all prepared specially for brewers and winemakers. The first two are quite quick-acting, producing results almost immediately, but these results are somewhat variable, and homebrewers seem to prefer chips or cubes, which are available in the form of both American and French oak and at different levels of toast. For full extraction, the beer will need to sit on these for two to six weeks. You may also be able to obtain an infusion spiral, which is basically an oak stave cut in a spiral manner so as to give a maximum of surface area. Drop this in your beer and let it sit there for fifteen to twenty weeks to optimize flavor extraction. Sanitizing any wood product before adding it to the beer will likely result in removing some of those flavor compounds you want to get into the beer. But not sanitizing them may be a risk of another color! If you are the sort who is afraid to dry-hop beer, then you had better sanitize the wood you put in it. If you are not afraid to dry-hop, then drop your oak in the fermenter and good luck!

However, it occurs to me while I write this that if you want to simulate aging in a used bourbon barrel, there might be another way. One of the main chemicals extracted from oak during aging is vanillin, which itself can be leached from vanilla beans by leaching with alcohol. So why not make your own vanilla extract, using bourbon rather than vodka, as I mentioned earlier? Then you can add this in controlled amounts to a sample of the beer, and scale up the addition for the main batch. No wood, no sanitation question, no variability in flavor, no brainer! All comments on this thought must be accompanied by a used $20 bill.

MAKING YOUR OWN AMBER AND BROWN MALT

There are advantages to making your own specialty malts, the first being that freshly roasted malt has a better, fuller flavor and aroma than one that is months, or even over a year, old. This perhaps matters less with very high-roast malts, such as black and chocolate, but certainly applies to brown and amber malt. And, of course, you will have the satisfaction of making it yourself, and to adjust the process so as to produce malts that are uniquely your own. Below is an approach to making your own brown and amber malts, which I have often used. The methodology owes something to that published by the Durden Park Beer Circle (*Old British Beers and How to Make Them,* 1991), but is somewhat modified and is the actual procedure I used. I am grateful to Durden Park for their permission to publish these procedures. Note that the temperature settings given are those recorded on a thermometer (thermocouple type). Settings on the cooker dial may not be as accurate, but should be close enough for practical purposes. However, it would be wise before you start to do a check against a thermometer for at least one setting, say 250°F (121°C), just to be sure.

AMBER MALT PROCEDURE:

Set the oven to 185°F (85°C), then take five pounds (2.3 kg) of pale malt (preferably Maris Otter variety) and place it in a shallow pan. Spread it as evenly as possible in the pan to a depth of about one inch; use a smaller amount if necessary so that you do not exceed this depth. Place it in the oven for twenty-five minutes, then set the temperature to 190°F (88°C) and leave for thirty minutes. Raise settings in steps at 200°F (93°C), 220°F (104°C), 230°F (110°C), and 250°F (121°C), allowing a twenty-five to thirty minute rest at each setting. At this point take a number of corns (fifteen to twenty) and break or cut them; they should have a very pale brown or buff color when compared to a sample of the starting pale malt. This is then the lowest color level for amber malt, and can be used as such in a brew. In order to develop the full color, continue at 250°F (121°C) for forty-five minutes or so, until the grain samples show a definite pale brown color, which is about the maximum color for amber malt. If you have a few grains of commercial amber malt, use these for color comparison, rather than pale malt. Let cool and store in an airtight container until used.

BROWN MALT PROCEDURE:

Proceed exactly as above, making a color comparison only after reaching the final amber malt stage. Raise the setting to 300°F (149°C) and maintain it for thirty minutes. Then raise the setting to 350°F (177°C) for twenty minutes and check for color as above, preferably against grains of commercial brown malt. If the color has reached a definite brown (but light as in "brown

Phil Markowski, head brewer at Two Roads Brewery, Stratford, Connecticut.

Source: Author

bag"), you're done. If it seems still to be pale, continue heating for another twenty minutes, but no more. Allow to cool and keep in an airtight container until used for brewing.

You could, of course, try your hand at making other specialty malts, such as crystal or caramel, and so on. I do not give any methods for that here, simply because I have not yet tried to do so myself. Just be warned that if you go for high-roast malts, such as chocolate and black, there is a very serious risk of fire, so these are perhaps best left to the experts!

CHAPTER FOUR

THE OTHER INGREDIENTS

THE RAW MATERIALS I DEALT WITH IN THE LAST CHAPTER MAINLY go to produce the wort. Now we need to look at further flavoring of the wort (hops), turning it into beer (yeast), and the base for the wort (brewing water).

Jeff Browning, brewer at BrüRm@BAR, New Haven, Connecticut.

HOPS

In many American craft beers and homebrews, hops are often thought of as being the most important ingredient. They are important in stouts and porters, but not in the same way as they are in pale ales, IPAs, double IPAs, pilsners, and so on. This is because in stouts and porters, with the exception of American stout, the hops are mainly there to provide bitterness only; flavor and aroma from hops is not, and need not be, apparent. Therefore, you could argue that in order to avoid creating large amounts of trub, with consequent loss of wort, we should use the minimum amount of hops possible. In other words, we should add only high alpha acid hops, and then only at the beginning of the boil. I would also say that we should use only pellet hops, because whatever the virtues of cone hops might be, they would be lost in this kind of beer. That does not mean that you cannot add flavor hops in a stout at the end of the boil, just that it should be done carefully so as not to smother the other flavors, especially in porters. Of course, it is your beer, and you can add whatever amount of hops wherever you like in the process, but the final beer might not be recognizable as a stout or porter! So in Table 4.1, I have listed some of the hops I recommend for stout and porter brewing (others will be suggested in the Recipe chapter).

I have listed US and UK hops separately, merely for convenience, not preference. However, if you were striving to be authentic in your porter/stout brewing, then you might want to use EK Goldings or Fuggles, since they are the oldest known English varieties still in production. If you wanted to add some hops late in the boil, I would suggest that you first consider those in Table 4.1 that come in at around 7 alpha-acid or below. Also, before selecting a late hop, think carefully about the characteristics of that particular style, and make sure that none of them will be subdued, or even obliterated, by the variety you have in mind for this addition. In Table 4.2, I offer a somewhat different approach, but bear in mind these are only suggestive and not exclusive.

4.1. A Selection of Hops Recommended for Brewing Stouts and Porters

Hop variety	Source	Typical* alpha acid range %	Hop Variety	Source	Typical alpha acid range %
Tomahawk	US	15–17	Admiral	UK	13.5–16
Warrior	US	15–17	Target	UK	9.5–12.5
Newport	US	13–17	Pilgrim	UK	9–13
Columbus	US	11–16	Phoenix	UK	8–12
Magnum	US	13–15	Northdown	UK	7.5–9.5
Horizon	US	11–14	Challenger	UK	6.5–8.5
Galena	US	10–14	First Gold	UK	6.5–8.5
Chinook	US	10–14	Progress	UK	5–7.5
Centennial	US	8–11.5	WGV**	UK	5–7
Bullion	US	6.5–9	E. Kent Goldings	UK	4–5.5
N. Brewer	US	6–10	Fuggles	UK	4–5.5
Perle	US	6–9.5%			
Mt. Hood	US	5–8			
Goldings	US	4–6			
Glacier	US	4–6			

*Typical means exactly what it says; in a particular year, any given variety might fall outside the typical range. Always check with your supplier to make sure you have the number for the sample actually in your hand!

**Whitbread Golding Variety is actually a Fuggles derivative.

Table 4.2 Hop Recommendations for Porters and Stouts			
Beer	**IBU**	**IBU/OG**	**Hop variety**
brown porter	20–30	0.6	N. Brewer, Galena, Columbus, Challenger, Fuggles, WGV
robust porter	30–45	0.7–0.8	N. Brewer, Warrior, Chinook, Target, Progress, Fuggles, US Goldings
Baltic porter	25–40	0.4–0.5	Perle, Mount Hood, EK Goldings, Target
dry stout	30–40	0.8–0.9	Fuggles, Northern Brewer, Magnum, Columbus, Bullion
foreign extra stout	40–70	1–1.1	Fuggles, Northern Brewer, Magnum, Tomahawk, Admiral, Bullion
sweet stout	15–30	N/A	Mount Hood, US and EK Goldings, Fuggles, Glacier
oatmeal stout	25–40	0.6–0.7	Columbus, Centennial, Mount Hood, North-down, WGV
American stout	45–70	0.8–1.0	Centennial, Chinook, Columbus, Horizon, Newport, Tomahawk[*]
Imperial stout	45–90	0.5–1	Warrior, Newport, Horizon, Galena, Target, Centennial, Chinook

[*]For American stout, you do want to go over the top and emphasize the hops, so late hopping is advisable, preferably with a citrusy American variety. That applies to most of the US hops listed in table 4.2, but I would also recommend Amarillo and Simcoe, not to mention that perennial favorite of American brewers, Cascade.

In order to determine how much of any given hop variety you need, if we assume that we are adding only bittering hops at the start of the boil, then we can use the simple equation:

$$IBU = \frac{(W \times \alpha \times U \times 0.749)}{BV}$$

Where W = weight of hops in ounces,
     α = alpha-acid percent (as a whole number),
     U = utilization (how much of the alpha-acid added gets through to the finished beer, and
     BV = beer volume in US gallons.

This is a simple equation, directly derived from the definition of IBU, and as it stands, applies to any hop addition. The main source of error in using it comes in the factor U, the utilization. That can only be found with any precision by actually measuring the IBU level in a given beer, using a relatively complicated spectrophotometric method and back-solving the equation for U. Even that only works for a single hop addition, and with that beer only, because U varies according to the wort gravity, when the hops were added in the boil, and how many iso-alpha acids (the true bittering factors) are lost mechanically during processes like fermentation. There are other equations in the homebrewing literature that attempt to take account of these variables, the most successful one apparently being that devised by Glenn Tinseth, which can easily be found on the web (if all else fails, go to www.rooftopbrew.net).

However, with porters and stouts, we are only talking about a single addition at the start of the boil, so if we can make a reasonable guess at U, then the equation is quite useful. In fact, it seems that a reasonable figure for this variable is around 20 to 25 percent, perhaps even less for worts of very high gravity, such as in Imperial stout brewing. A practical approach, and one that I generally follow, is to assume 25 percent utilization, take the target IBU, and use the equation to calculate the required addition of the chosen hop variety. If the bitterness level in the beer is not where I want it to be, then I simply adjust the addition rate accordingly for the next version of it. If you prefer, you can take the even simpler practical approach and use alpha acid units (AAU). These are just the weight of hops, in ounces, multiplied by their alpha-acid percent as a whole number. This doesn't give you any direct estimate of the IBU level, but again gives you a basis from which to make comparisons, and to adjust the addition rate on the next go at brewing the same beer. It also gives you a good guide as to how much to add when switching from one hop to another, if you want to experiment with different varieties.

There is an exception to what I said at the start of the last paragraph, and that is American stouts, where hops will be added later in the boil, and not just at the start for bittering. Observations from several commercial brewers have indicated that even those hops added at the end of the boil will contribute significantly to bitterness. One brewer, for example, states that 15 to 20 percent hop utilization is achieved with hops added at the start of whirlpooling after the boil. What the homebrewer might get is debatable, for it depends upon

Ca. 1902 workers and a coopered storage vat at the Cremo Brewing Co. in New Britain, Connecticut.

whether you use a whirlpool, how long your post-boil stand is, and so on. This is a topic that is really beyond the scope of this book, so all I will say here is that for American stouts, I shall assume the conservative figure of 10 percent utilization for late added hops. I shall refer to this again in the notes at the start of the Recipe chapter.

This relatively short section is all I am going to say about hops in porters and stouts, since their effect on these beers is limited. With the exception of American stout, it's the malt flavors that count most.

YEAST

Well, it's not only the malt flavors that count, because the yeast strain used also affects the final flavor of porter or stout. And in contrast to when I wrote my earlier book on porter, we now have an abundance of different yeast strains to choose from. The widest selection comes from the two suppliers of liquid yeasts, White Labs and Wyeast, but there is also a reasonable choice among dry yeasts. And of course, with the presence of so many craft brewers in this country, you also have the

Table 4.3 Suggested Yeast Strains for Porters and Stouts.			
Beer Style	WYEAST liquid	White Labs liquid	Dry Yeasts
brown porter	1028 London Ale 1098 British Ale 1275 Thames Valley Ale 1056 American Ale	002 English Ale 006 Bedford British 001 California Ale	SAFALE S04 SAFALE US-05 Munton's Ale
robust porter	1028 London Ale 1099 Whitbread Ale* 1275 Thames Valley Ale	002 English Ale 005 British Ale 013 London Ale	DANSTAR Nottingham Ale Munton's Ale
Baltic porter**	2112 California Lager*** 2633 Octoberfest Lager Blend	810 San Francisco Lager*** 820 Oktoberfest Lager	Saflager S-23 Brewferm Lager Saflager W-34/70

Continued

dry stout	1084 Irish Ale 1187 Ringwood Ale**** 1335 British Ale II	004 Irish Ale 002 English Ale 023 Burton Ale	DANSTAR Windsor Ale SAFBREW S33
foreign extra stout	1084 Irish Ale 1728 Scottish Ale 1056 American Ale	004 Irish Ale 028 Edinburgh Ale 041 Pacific Ale	SAFALE S04 Cooper's Ale
sweet stout	1968 London ESB Ale 1318 London Ale III	013 London Ale 028 Edinburgh Ale	SAFALE US-05 DANSTAR Windsor Ale
oatmeal stout	1099 Whitbread Ale 1028 London Ale 1084 Irish Ale	002 English Ale 013 London Ale 004 Irish Ale	SAFALE S04 Munton's Ale
American stout	1272 American Ale II 1056 American Ale 1098 British Ale	051 California Ale V 060 American Ale Blend 008 East Coast Ale	SAFALE US-05 DANSTAR Nottingham Ale
Imperial stout*****	1728 Scottish Ale 1272 American Ale II 1028 London Ale	007 Dry English 028 Edinburgh Ale 060 American Ale Blend	DANSTAR Nottingham Ale SAFBREW S33

*White Labs also offers WLP017 Whitbread Ale Yeast, but on a seasonal basis only.

**I have listed lager yeasts, which may require cold fermentation at around 50°F (10°C).

***Just to contradict myself, these strains can be fermented as high as 65°F (18.3°C), and will still give "lager-like" flavors.

****The Ringwood strain is an eccentric one, and can give high levels of esters and of diacetyl. Do not ferment above 65°F (18.3°C), and when primary fermentation is complete, keep at 65°F to 70°F (18.3°C to 21.1°C) to reduce diacetyl.

*****Since you want to achieve good attenuation to avoid a too sweet Imperial Stout, also consider looking at one or two of the Belgian ale yeasts, such as Wyeast 3787 Trappist High Gravity, or WLP500Trappist Ale.

possibility of obtaining supplies of fresh, active yeast from one near you. So in Table 4.3 above are my suggestions for yeast strains for the nine beer styles we are dealing with.

The strains I have listed are mostly similar, but not identical, and my choices are quite subjective and based on my own experience. I have not given any of the properties of these strains or of any other available strains, since I do not have the space here to do so. In any case, you will find all the information you need on the Internet, notably at www.wyeastlab.com and www.whitelabs.com/. When you choose a yeast strain, do remember to bear in mind what you want to achieve with it for the particular beer you are brewing. At this point, I should make a comment about making soured versions of any of these beers. If you are going to try to reproduce an "original" porter or stout, you might want to use a *Brettanomyces* strain, making the assumption that these early beers would have come up against this yeast during long storage in wood. If you decide to do this, you should go with *Brettanomyces clausennii*, which is the species that was first isolated from English Stock Ales by Claussen in the early twentieth century. Brett species of Belgium origin are likely to give you a much more sour beer than you bargained for!

For all these beers, except Baltic porters brewed using a low-temperature fermenting lager strain, your fermentations can be carried out at "warm" temperatures of 65°F to 70°F (18.3°C to 21.1°C). Secondary fermentation is optional, but generally desirable, as it helps not only to clear the beer, but also to ensure good control of diacetyl levels. Note that making a starter is essential for the higher gravity worts, and particularly so for Baltic porters if you are using a low temperature fermentation.

One of the most common mistakes made by homebrewers is that of under pitching the yeast. It is not appropriate at this point to give you a dissertation on how to work out the amount you need to pitch. There are two handy sources which will help you to do this: www.mrmalty.com/ offers a very comprehensive pitching rate calculator, and there is also a somewhat more simplified version available on the

Wyeast website. If you do not want to do that, follow my rough guidelines for liquid yeasts as given in the next paragraph.

For a wort of SG up to 1.060 (14.7°P), a starter of one to one and a half quarts (about 1 to 1.5L) made from one vial or one smash pack should be fine. But at higher gravities, you will need at least two vials or packs made into separate one-quart (1L) starters. For the biggest Imperial stouts at 1.090 (21.5°P) or more, you should use at least three vials or packs, and the same for a big Baltic porter, especially if it is brewed with a lager yeast at lower temperatures. If you think that is going to cost too much, just think what it will cost you if you spend all that effort and money to brew an Imperial stout, and it is virtually undrinkable because it hasn't fermented out and is too sweet!

To make the starter, you can use a malt extract syrup, and aim for a wort OG of around 1.040 (10°P), which is about one pound of syrup per gallon. Use a hopped syrup for convenience, and dissolve it in water, then make up to one gallon (assuming we are going to brew a high gravity beer; for lower gravity beers, just one to two quarts will suffice). Boil the wort for twenty to thirty minutes, cool to around 70°F (21°C), transfer to a sterile jar, and pitch the yeast from the two or three vials or smash packs (having activated the latter as per the instructions), then seal the jar with cling film, or with cotton wool if it has a narrow neck. For best results, oxygenate the wort before pitching the yeast. Leave in a warm area for two days, when a good layer of sediment should be visible in the jar. You have to plan all this ahead so that the starter is ready when the main wort is ready. Decant as much of the starter liquid as possible, swirl the remainder about so as to loosen the sediment, then pitch it in the main wort, which should have first been thoroughly oxygenated. I like to use separate one-quart (1L) jars, since this will tell me if there are any problems with the individual vials or packs.

If you are using dried yeast, you may want to take a slightly different approach and not use a starter at all. One packet is fine for beers of OG below 1.060 (14.7°P), but I would still add two packets for beers of higher starting gravity. Opinion seems to be divided as to whether dried yeast should be sprinkled directly onto the wort, or whether it should first be rehydrated in warm water at around 100°F (38°C), so I leave that decision to you. The packs generally contain around 10g of dried yeast, which is a fair amount, so it is also debatable as to whether a starter is required. I still prefer to make a starter, since doing so is a good check on the viability of the yeast cells in your particular pack, as well as a means of ensuring that you achieve an adequate pitching rate.

WATER

It is well known that many beer styles evolved at particular locations because of the chemistry of the local brewing water. Just think of Burton on Trent and IPA, London and Dublin for stouts and porters, Munich for dark lagers, and Plzen for pilsner. Of course, in the eighteenth and nineteenth centuries, water chemistry and its effects on brewing were not well understood, whereas nowadays we can brew any style of beer anywhere by making appropriate adjustments to the water. The key is that of mash acidity (measured as pH); the water at a particular place mentioned above was suited to a particular beer because it would result in the right mash pH to ensure optimum yield of fermentables from the malt. We do not need to worry about that too much with stouts and porters, because the quality of modern base malts is such that pH is not so critical in obtaining a high yield of extract. Also, our beers are brewed with roasted malts, which themselves play a role in controlling mash pH. However, this is life, and things are not always that simple, and there are a couple of points to consider about brewing water. But don't worry, I won't get into any really complicated chemistry. Just in case you want to do so, I suggest you read the relevant chapter in Greg Noonan's *New Brewing Lager Beer,* available from Brewers Publications.

The first point is to discover whether you have chlorine and/or chloramines in your water supply. That is pretty likely, since these are chemicals commonly used by utilities to treat the water before sending it out for public use. Just how much your supply contains of chloramines and chlorine can be found out by asking for an analysis from your supplier. If these chemicals are present in your water supply, they can cause the formation of off flavors in your beer, especially from the formation of chlorophenols, so it is preferable to remove them. Chlorine is relatively easy to remove by boiling the brew water before use, which I tend to do as part of my brewing routine. Chloramines are a little more difficult to get rid of, however. Some brewers have done so by adding Campden tablets (potassium metabisulfite), which can be obtained from your usual homebrew retailer. Most likely you'll need only about one such tablet per twenty gallons (75L), but a much better approach is to install an activated carbon filter before the faucet from which you draw your brewing water. They are inexpensive and relatively easy to install, and if it is used only for brewing water, you will not have to change the cartridge very often. Even one fitted to the supply for the kitchen will only require changing about every six months or so, and a new cartridge only costs a few dollars. As a matter of fact, I installed one in our kitchen that has dramatically improved the flavor of our coffee!

The other potential problem is a lack of bicarbonate ions in the water. So what? Well, bicarbonates, as salts of a weak acid, have what is known as a buffering effect. This means that they tend to thwart the effects of stronger acids, and to prevent them from lowering the pH of the mash. That means that their presence is bad if you want to make a pale beer, because they will tend to make the pH stay above the optimum range of 5.2 to 5.5, which will reduce extract efficiency and make the flavor "flabby." But the presence of bicarbonate ions is good if you are making a dark beer using acidic roasted malts, because these ions will prevent the pH from falling below 5.2 to 5.5. It is no accident that the two great centers for brewing porters and stouts were London and Dublin, where the waters used for brewing had relatively high bicarbonate contents.

Are you with me so far? Good, then what happens when you brew a stout with water that contains little or no bicarbonates? It is quite simple—roasted malts, especially black malt, being somewhat acidic, will drive the pH down, possibly below pH 5.2. That will spoil your extraction efficiency, but perhaps even more importantly, may result in a beer that is so acidic that it has a sour edge. This may not be much of a problem with porters, where there may be little or no black malt in the grist, but it certainly will be with stouts using relatively large amounts of black malt, and especially with dry stouts, much of whose main coloring and flavor comes from that malt. But first, let's invoke the KISS Principle (or use Occam's razor, if you prefer) and take the simple approach. If the utility analysis shows the presence of bicarbonates, and if you have brewed stouts and had no problem like this, then you do not need to make any adjustments. But if the water has no bicarbonate content and your dry stout has been proven to taste rather acidic, rather than sharp and clean, then you do need to change things. The first thing you should do is to buy a pH meter (they're not too expensive these days) and check the pH of your stout mash the next time you brew it. If it is below pH 5.2, you have a problem and must add some carbonate. Oh, and I almost forgot, even if your water does contain bicarbonates, if you have boiled it to remove chlorine, you will also have reduced the bicarbonate content, since this precipitates out as calcium carbonate.

The advantage of having your own pH meter is that you won't need to bother with complicated chemical calculations. Simply check the mash pH and add either calcium or sodium carbonate until you have got it in the right range of pH 5.2 to 5.5. The best way to do this is to draw off a measured volume, say 100mL, and add small amounts of carbonate while stirring, let it sit for two to three minutes, and recheck the mash pH. Continue to do this until it reaches pH 5.2. Total your added amounts, multiply up to the scale of the whole mash, and add this calculated amount of carbonate to the whole mash, allowing a few minutes before checking again to see that you've got it right. And naturally, you must take notes and make the same total adjustment on the next stout you brew. I prefer to add calcium carbonate, since this also furnishes calcium ions, which are beneficial in several aspects of the brewing process. And be quite clear—you cannot adjust the water in this way, as calcium carbonate is insoluble in water; it must be added to the mash itself.

Note that the above applies to all-grain brews, and extract brewers should not have to worry too much about treating their water, as this will have been done by the manufacturers in making the original mash prior to evaporation of the wort. However, you may need to check the pH of any partial mash you are doing, and make adjustments as appropriate. But back to KISS, and let your taste buds make the choice. If your first shots at stouts, especially the dry versions, gave a good, clean, and sharp bite with no unpleasant acidity, just keep on doing what you have been doing!

FININGS

These naturally derived chemicals are often overlooked by homebrewers, but should be considered in brewing porters and stouts. Most important of these is **carrageenan,** or **Irish moss,** a seaweed product. Carrageenan is an unusual polysaccharide molecule in that it carries a strong negative charge from sulfate groups on some of the sugar rings. That makes them capable of adsorbing onto the materials of trub, forming large flocs that can settle well and form a tightly bound mass in the kettle, so that the beer can easily be run off or siphoned off from the trub. Irish moss comes in the form of flaked seaweed and is dosed at the rate of one teaspoon per five-gallon (19L) brew, and is added about twenty minutes before the end of the boil. Personally, I have found results somewhat inconsistent with this material, and I much prefer the purified, processed form, which comes as a tablet under various trade names, such as Whirlfloc and Koppakleer. These are used as directed, usually at the rate of half a tablet per five gallons (19L), added in the last few minutes of the boil. Using copper finings is not essential, but is good insurance against excessive loss of wort to the trub, and helps to minimize trub carryover into the fermenter.

The other forms of finings are **gelatin** and **isinglass,** which are both proteinaceous materials and are used to flocculate yeast. That is, they are big molecules that adsorb onto the yeast particles, forming flocs, which settle more readily than the yeast does so unaided. Gelatin is a lower molecular weight polymer than isinglass and forms smaller tighter flocs than the latter. These flocs settle rather slowly, and in my opinion offer little advantage when used in either bottled or kegged beer, unless you are going to filter it. Gelatin is used at the rate of one-quarter to one-half teaspoon per five gallons (19L) of beer, added to the bulk just before bottling or kegging. It has to first be dissolved in about one cup of very hot water, with vigorous stirring to ensure that it is fully dissolved.

Isinglass forms much larger flocs and is very effective in settling most yeast strains. You can buy it as a powder and make your own solution, which you add to the beer at the rate of three to four ounces (100 to 120mL) of a 1 percent solution per five gallons (19L) of beer. However, it is much simpler to buy it as a prepared solution and add it at the rate recommended by the supplier. It probably isn't very useful if you are bottling, since the yeast has to settle only a small distance and will do so on its own, given two or three weeks settling time. I find it useful for kegged beers, since it forms a firm sediment, which will readily resettle if the keg is disturbed in any way. Its prime use is in fining cask-conditioned beers, and it is widely used in England by commercial brewers for that purpose.

An unusual name for a brewpub.

CHAPTER FIVE

BREWING PORTERS AND STOUTS—RECIPES

INTRODUCTION

A series of recipes for each style will follow this, including all-grain and extract-based beers, with an equal number of recipes for each method. Following that will be ten more recipes of special interest, as will be explained in the notes on each one. In developing all these, I have made a number of assumptions and recommendations:

1. All recipes are for a finished volume of five US gallons (19L). I have given percentages of the total, as well as actual weights, in order to help you understand how the recipes were formulated.

2. Grain yields are based on 65 percent brew house efficiency. If your efficiency is higher

Ron Page, brewer at City Steam Brewpub, Hartford, Connecticut.

(or lower), then simply multiply down (or up) on the amounts given in the recipe by the ratio of your efficiency to the 65 percent baseline.

3. Malt extract recipes are based on yields of 1.036 SG/lb./gallon for liquid extracts, and 1.045 SG/lb./gallon for dried malt extracts. Separate instructions are given if grain steeping or partial mashing is required for extract recipes.

4. Mash times are ninety minutes, unless otherwise stated, and I have used a water-to-grain ratio of 1.25 quarts per pound. At the end of mashing, wort collection and sparging should be carried out to give a final boil volume of 5.5 to six gallons (21 to 23L).

5. Boil times are ninety minutes for all-grain recipes, and sixty minutes for extract-based recipes. In the latter case, a full wort boil is assumed; if you boil smaller amounts, you will have to adjust hop rates to allow for lower extraction of α-acids.

6. All hop rates are based on the use of pelletized hops only; for bittering purposes you should add about 10 percent more if you are using cone hops.

7. In calculating IBU levels a 25 percent utilization of α-acids. is assumed. For those who prefer it, I have also given hop dosage as alpha acid units (AAU). In the case of American stouts, I shall give two figures, one for the hops added at the start of the boil, and in brackets after that, the total to be expected if the late hops give 10 percent utilization (as discussed in Other Ingredients chapter).

8. The color levels given are based on the sum of the proportionate contribution of all malts according to their assumed SRM values. In other words, SRM × weight in lb./5 (gallons). This calculation is for comparative purposes only and does not indicate actual color of the beer in SRM, which is also influenced by caramelization during boiling. There may be a direct relation between this calculated color and SRM, but I am unaware of one that is suitable for the dark colors of stouts and porters. Note also SRM values given for malt extracts are rather uncertain, since information from the manufacturers is somewhat limited, so in some instances the Lovibond number I have given is little more than an educated guess.

9. Fermentation should be carried out at 65°F to 70°F (18.3°C to 21.1°C) unless otherwise noted. Yeast will generally be added as a starter for best results. For lower strength beers—that is, those below about OG 1.060 (14.7°P)—a one-quart (1L) starter from one pack of liquid or dried yeast is fine. For bigger beers, you need at least two packs of yeast and a starter of at least two quarts (1.9L), and you should consider doubling that when using a lager yeast for the biggest Baltic porters, which are fermented with a lager yeast at cool temperatures (of the order of 40 to 45°F or 4.4 to 7.2°C). Note that you do not use the *entire* starter; decant off most of the liquid and add the sediment to your wort.

10. Most of these beers will benefit from racking to a secondary fermenter at room temperature for one to three weeks before racking to bottle or keg. This makes it easier to ensure good clarity in the finished beer, and to ensure almost complete removal of diacetyl. The strongest beers, such as the Imperial stouts, will be improved by longer term maturation, months or even years depending upon the beer. However, in that case, such maturation should be carried out at cool temperatures, say around 40°F (4.4°C), so as to reduce the harmful effects of oxidation.

11. Priming and carbonation should be carried out by your usual method; this will be discussed further after the recipe chapter.

12. In the recipes, I have usually recommended specific malts, yeasts, and hops. These are *not* cast in stone, and you are welcome and even encouraged to use equivalent alternatives according to your taste and what may be available to you. In the case of bittering hops, you should adjust the amount if those you are using have a different α-content to those I have quoted. Note that in those recipes where no source is given for a particular ingredient, the choice is entirely yours!

Finally, you may find some repetition in the instruction going from one recipe to another. This is not carelessness on my part, but rather a deliberate attempt to make each recipe "self-sufficient," and capable of being read (and followed) without reference to other recipes.

BROWN PORTERS

Straight-Up Porter

(all-grain)

Ingredients

8.5 lb. (3.9 kg) US two-row pale malt (2°L); 85%
1.0 lb. (454 g) UK crystal malt (60°L); 10%
0.5 lb. (227 g) Crisp chocolate malt (450°L); 5%
1 oz. (28 g) US Northern Brewer pellets, 9% AA (9 AAU, 90 min.)
Wyeast 1028 London Ale; White Labs WLP 002 English Ale

Original gravity: 1.049 (12.2°P)
Final gravity: 1.010 (2.6°P)
ABV: 5.1%
IBU: 34
SRM: 60

Directions

Mash at 152°F to 154°F (66.7°C to 67.8°C) with 12 quarts (11.5L) of water; mature two to three weeks.

Notes

Simple to do, smooth yet slightly chewy, but easy to drink! An option is to add a vanilla bean at the end of the boil; this will add a nice little extra zing. I don't need to explain the name, do I?

Napoleon Brownaparte

(all-grain)

Ingredients

3.75 lb. (1.7 kg) UK two-row pale malt (3°L); 33.3%
3.75 lb. (1.7 kg) Crisp brown malt (65°L); 33.3%
3.75 lb. (1.7 kg) Crisp amber malt (29°L); 33.3%

1.5 oz. (43 g) UK Goldings pellets, 5% AA (7.5 AAU, 90 min.)
Wyeast 1098 British Ale; White Labs WLP 006 Bedford Ale

Original gravity: 1.052 (12.9°P)
Final gravity: 1.016 (4.1°P)
ABV: 4.6%
IBU: 28
SRM: 73

Directions
Mash at 150°F (65.6°C) with 14 quarts (13L) of water; mature two to three weeks.

Notes
A traditional recipe, as was often used in the early nineteenth century. You can make it perhaps even more traditional with a hint of smoke by replacing 0.5 pounds (227 g) of amber malt with the same amount of peated malt. Do not make big changes from the above, which is a very well-balanced beer. I don't know where I got the name, because I always think of a pig when I hear "Napoleon," simply because of the character in *Animal Farm*, written by one of my favorite authors, George Orwell.

Mildly Multinational
(all-grain)

Ingredients
7.0 lb. (3.2 kg) UK mild ale malt (4°L); 59.6%
2.5 lb. (1.1 kg) Briess Munich malt (10°L); 21.3%
1.0 lb. (454 g) Briess Carabrown® WK brown malt (55°L); 8.5%
1.0 lb. (454 g) Belgian Special B malt (140°L); 8.5%
0.25 lb.(113 g) Weyermann Rye malt (3°L); 2.1%
0.8 oz. (23 g) Columbus pellets, 10% AA (8 AAU, 90 min.)
Wyeast 1056 American Ale; White Labs WLP 001 California Ale

Original gravity: 1.055 (13.6°P)
Final gravity: 1.015 (3.8°P)
ABV: 5.2%
IBU: 30
SRM: 50

Directions
Mash at 154°F (67.8°C) with 15 quarts (14L) of water; mature two to three weeks.

Notes
This one is more complex and "modern" than the first two versions, with a high mash temperature to give extra body and bready and spicy notes from the Special B and rye malts, but still balanced. A good option to add another dimension to the flavor would be to add 25 grams of licorice for the last half hour of wort boiling. The name just reflects the use of ingredients from a variety of sources.

Moving On Porter

(extract plus steeped grains)

Ingredients
6.0 lb. (2.7 kg) Cooper's amber malt syrup (15°L); 85.7%
0.5 lb. (227 g) Baird chocolate malt (450°L); 7.1%
0.5 lb. (227 g) UK crystal malt (80°L); 7.1%
2.0 oz. (57 g) UK Fuggles pellets, 4% AA (8 AAU, 60 min.)
Wyeast 1028 London Ale; White Labs WLP 005 British Ale

Original gravity: 1.048 (11.9°P)
Final gravity: 1.011 (2.8°P)
ABV: 4.8%
IBU: 30
SRM: 71

Directions

Steep grains in 2 quarts (1.9L) hot water at around 160°F (71.1°C), strain and rinse thoroughly using two lots of 2 quarts (1.9L) of hot water. Use liquor for dissolving extract and top up with water to boil volume. Mature the brew for two to three weeks.

Notes

A straightforward porter formulated on the KISS principle; luscious yet with a hint of roast from the chocolate malt, and with a beautiful red-brown color. Go for the extra flavor of vanilla if you think this recipe is too simple! The name? Well, it just seemed right in moving on from all-grain to an extract recipe for the first time in this chapter.

Simple Simon Says

(extract only)

Ingredients

6.6 lb. (3.0 kg) Briess CBW Porter malt syrup (17°L); 93%
0.5 lb. (227 g) Briess CBW Traditional Dark DME (30°L); 7%
1.5 oz. (43 g) UK WGV pellets, 6% AA (9 AAU, 60 min.)
Wyeast 1028 London Ale; White Labs WLP 013 London Ale

Original gravity: 1.052 (12.9°P)
Final gravity: 1.014 (3.6°P)
ABV: 4.9%
IBU: 34
SRM: 80

Directions

Dissolve syrup and DME in 3 gallons (11L) warm water, make to boil volume with warm water. Mature the brew for two to three weeks.

Notes

Even simpler than the previous version, yet still a tasty beer and one well worth drinking; 25 grams of licorice added to the last half hour of the boil would provide a little more complexity of flavor. The name reflects the construction of the recipe.

Brown Bear Porter

(extract plus partial mash)

Ingredients

6.0 lb. (2.7 kg) Munton's amber malt syrup (30°L); 70.6%
1.0 lb. (454 g) US 2-row pale malt (2°L); 11.8%
1.0 lb. (454 g) Crisp brown malt (65°L); 11.8%
0.5 lb. (227 g) Belgian biscuit malt (25°L); 5.9%
1.0 oz. (28 g) Challenger pellets, 7% AA (7 AAU, 60 min.)
Wyeast 1099 Whitbread Ale; White Labs WLP 002 English Ale

Original gravity: 1.055 (13.6°P)
Final gravity: 1.016 (4.1°P)
ABV: 5.1%
IBU: 26
SRM: 52

Directions

Mash grains at 150°F to 152°F (65.6°C to 66.7°C) with 3 quarts (3L) water for 45 minutes, strain and rinse thoroughly with two lots of 3 quarts (3L) hot water. Use liquor to dissolve syrup and top up to boil volume with water. Mature the brew for two to three weeks.

Notes

A beer more like a traditional than a modern porter, with extra layers of flavor from the brown and biscuit malts. The partial mash means more effort, but I think you will find it worthwhile when you drink this beer. The derivation of the name should be obvious.

ROBUST PORTERS

Black, Brown, and Beige Porter

(all-grain)

Ingredients

10.0 lb. (4.5 kg) UK mild ale malt (4°L); 87%
0.75 lb. (340 g) Briess caramel malt (60°L); 6.5%
0.5 lb. (227 g) Briess 2-row chocolate malt (350°L); 4.3%
0.25 lb. (113 g) Simpson black malt (550°L); 2.2%
1.2 oz. (34 g) US Northern Brewer pellets, 9% AA (10.8 AAU, 90 min.)
Wyeast 1028 London Ale; White Labs WLP 013 London Ale

Original gravity: 1.055 (13.6°P)
Final gravity: 1.012 (3.1°P)
ABV: 5.6%
IBU: 40
SRM: 80

Directions

Mash at 151°F to 153°F (66.1°C to 67.2°C), using 14 quarts (13.5 L) of water; mature the brew for two to three weeks.

Notes

This is a relatively modest robust porter with roasted notes mainly in the background, but the caramel malt and the relatively high mash temperature add some palate fullness. The name is a little bit of homage to the great Duke Ellington.

Victoria's Revelation Porter

(all-grain)

Ingredients

9.0 lb. (4.1 kg) Maris Otter pale malt (3°L); 71.7%
0.60 lb. (272 g) Vienna malt (4°L); 4.8%
0.60 lb. (272 g) Briess 2-row chocolate malt (350°L); 4.8%
0.60 lb. (113 g) Briess BlackPrinz® malt (500°L); 4.8%
1.75 lb. (0.8 kg) Crisp brown malt (65°L); 13.9%
2.5 oz. (71 g) US Goldings pellets, 5% AA (12.5 AAU, 90 min.)
Wyeast 1099 Whitbread Ale; White Labs WLP 005 British Ale

Original gravity: 1.060 (14.7°P)
Final gravity: 1.019 (4.8°P)
ABV: 5.3%
IBU: 47
SRM: 130

Directions

Mash at 150°F (65.6°C) using 16 quarts (15L) of water; mature the brew for three to four weeks.

Notes

This has definite roasted character, but muted because the black malt is de-bittered, and the palate is also modified by the licorice notes from the brown malt. Use of Vienna and Maris Otter adds a nice fullness to this beer. The name is a pun on that of a well-known retailer and the fact that this is a "Victorian" style porter.

Naughty But Nice Porter

(all-grain)

Ingredients

6.0 lb. (2.7 kg) Briess Ashburne® mild ale malt (5°L); 60%
1.0 lb. (454 g) Briess Munich malt (10°L); 10%

1.0 lb. (454 g) Crisp amber malt (29°L); 10%
1.0 lb. (454 g) Crisp brown malt (65°L); 10%
0.5 lb. (227 g) Briess Special Roast malt (63°L); 5%
0.25 lb.(113 g) Weyermann CARAFA I (340°L); 2.5%
0.25 lb.(113 g) Baird black malt (550°L); 2.5%
0.7 oz. (20 g) Chinook pellets, 11% AA (7.7 AAU, 90 min.)
Wyeast 1275 Thames Valley Ale; Munton's Ale

Original gravity: 1.046 (11.4°P)
Final gravity: 1.014 (3.6°P)
ABV: 4.1%
IBU: 29
SRM: 77

Directions
Mash at 150°F (65.6°C) using 13 quarts (12L) of water; mature the brew for two to three weeks.

Notes
Yes, roasted flavor is present, but backed by a range of other flavors, particularly those of nuttiness from amber, licorice from brown, chocolate from the CARAFA malt, and the bready character of the special roast malt. The mix of mild ale and Munich malts adds a slight background sweetness and body in this brew. The name is an adaptation of the famous catchphrase of a British TV comedian back in the 1960s and 1970s, so it probably won't mean much to you!

January Thaw Porter
(extract plus steeped grains)

Ingredients
6.0 lb. (2.7 kg) Munton amber malt syrup (30°L); 72.7%
1.5 lb. (680 g) Munton's DME (12°L); 18.2%
0.25 lb. (113 g) Briess BlackPrinz® malt (500°L); 3%
0.25 lb. (113 g) Munton chocolate malt (380°L); 3%

0.25 lb. (113 g) Belgian Special B malt (140°L); 3%
1.0 oz. (28 g) Warrior pellets, 14% AA (14 AAU, 60 min.)
White Labs WLP 005 British Ale, Nottingham Ale

Original gravity: 1.060 (14.7°P)
Final gravity: 1.016 (4.1°P)
ABV: 5.7%
IBU: 52
SRM: 91

Directions

Place grains in a muslin bag and steep them in 4 quarts (3.8L) hot water at around 160°F (71.1°C), strain and rinse thoroughly, using two 4-quart (3.8L) lots of hot water. Use liquor for dissolving extract and top up with water to boil volume. Mature the brew for three to four weeks.

Notes

This has a modest roasted character, but because of the de-bittered black malt, it is very well-rounded and drinkable. The Special B adds caramel and dried fruit flavors in the background to help the balance of the beer. It is another beer that might benefit from the addition of a vanilla bean or two in the last stages of the boil. The name comes from a common weather phenomenon here in Connecticut.

Fateful Dread Porter

(extract plus steeped grains)

Ingredients

6.0 lb. (2.7 kg) pale malt syrup (10°L); 72.7%
1.0 lb. (454 g) Briess caramel malt (80°L); 12.1%
0.5 lb. (227 g) Fawcett pale chocolate malt (200°L); 6%
0.5 lb. (227 g) Briess Special Roast malt (63°L); 6%

0.25 lb. (113 g) Simpson black malt (550°L); 3%
1.6 oz. (45 g) Progress pellets, 6% AA (9.6 AAU, 60 min.)
Wyeast 1028 British Ale, WLP002 English Ale

Original gravity: 1.053 (13.1°P)
Final gravity: 1.013 (3.3°P)
ABV: 5.2%
IBU: 36
SRM: 82

Directions

Place grains in a muslin bag and steep them in 4 quarts (3.8L) hot water at around 160°F (71.1°C); strain and rinse thoroughly, using two 4-quart (3.8L) lots of hot water at around 160°F (71.1°C). Use liquor for dissolving extract and top up with water to boil volume. Mature the brew for two to three weeks.

Notes

Just a hint of coffee from the black malt, with more of a pleasing fullness from the chocolate malt than roasted character, and some bready/biscuity flavors from the special roast malt. The name is an homage to another musician, and also reflects my love of word play.

Albert's Memorial Porter

(extract plus partial mash)

Ingredients

4.5 lb. (2.0 kg) amber malt syrup (30°L); 46.2%
2.0 lb. (910 g) US 2-row pale malt (2°L); 20.5%
1.0 lb. (454 g) Crisp amber malt (29°L); 10.3%
1.0 lb. (454 g) Briess Carabrown® WK brown malt (55°L); 10.3%
0.50 lb. (227 g) Belgian Biscuit malt (25°L); 5.1%
0.50 lb. (227 g) Briess Victory malt (28°L); 5.1

0.25 lb. (113 g) Briess BlackPrinz® malt (500°L)
2.5 oz. (71 g) US Fuggles pellets, 4.5% AA (11.3 AAU, 60 min.)
Wyeast 1275 Thames Valley Ale; Danstar Windsor Ale

Original gravity: 1.057 (14.0°P)
Final gravity: 1.015 (3.8°P)
ABV: 5.5%
IBU: 42
SRM: 75

Directions

Mash grains (in a muslin bag) with 1.5 gallons (5.7L) water at 150°F to 152°F (65.6°C to 66.7°C) for 45 minutes, strain and rinse twice with 1.5 gallons (5.7L) water each time. Use liquor to dissolve syrup, and increase to final volume with water before boiling. Mature the brew for two to three weeks.

Notes

This porter is a much more complex beer than its two predecessors, with lots of bready and licorice characters coming from the amber

Church Brewing, Pittsburgh, Pennsylvania.

brown and biscuit malts and competing with the harsher flavor of the black malt. It requires a rather big-scale partial mash, so you can lose out on OG if you do not do this very carefully. The extra effort is worth it, I can assure you! The name is a reference to Queen Victoria's husband, and suits a beer brewed during her reign.

BALTIC PORTERS

Tiger from Riga

(all-grain)

Ingredients

9.0 lb. (4.1 kg) US 2-row pale malt (2°L); 57.5%
3.0 lb. (1.4 kg) Briess Munich malt (10°L); 19.2%
2.0 lb. (910 g) Belgian Vienna malt (4°L); 12.8%
0.5 lb. (227 g) Belgian Special B malt (140°L); 3.2%
1.0 lb. (454 g) UK crystal malt (40°L); 6.4%
2.50 oz. (0.07 kg) Briess BlackPrinz® malt (500°L); 1%
1.0 oz. (28 g) Perle pellets, 8.0% AA (8 AAU, 90 min.)
Wyeast 2633 Octoberfest Blend; White Labs WLP820 Octoberfest Lager

Original gravity: 1.075 (18.2°P)
Final gravity: 1.020 (5.1°P)
ABV: 7.2%
IBU: 30
SRM: 49

Directions

Several days in advance, prepare yeast starter of at least 2 to 3 quarts (1.9 to 2.8L). Mash at 152°F to 153°F (66.7°C to 67°C), using 20 quarts (19L) of water. Pitch yeast starter into cooled wort and ferment at 40°F to 45°F (4.4°C to 7.2°C) for seven to ten days. Carry out a diacetyl rest at around 65°F (18.3°C) for a minimum of forty-eight hours before maturing for one to two months.

Notes

This brew is meant to be a smooth-drinking beer (hence the use of a de-bittered black malt), but with the variety of malts used, you will find there is a range of flavors as it rolls over the tongue. The name comes from an Edward Lear limerick about a Lady from Riga.

Tallinn Knights Porter

(all-grain)

Ingredients

10.0 lb. (4.5 kg) Weyermann Bohemian pilsner malt (2°L); 52.6%
5.0 lb. (2.3 kg) Briess Munich malt (10°L); 26.3%
2.0 lb. (910 g) Baird brown malt (58°L); 10.5%
1.0 lb. (454 g) Briess caramel malt (20°L); 5.3%
0.5 lb. (227 g) UK crystal malt (40°L); 2.6%
0.50 lb. (227 g) Fawcett pale chocolate malt (200°L); 2.6%
2.0 oz. (57 g) Mt. Hood pellets, 5.0% AA (10 AAU, 90 min.)
Wyeast 2112 California Lager; White Labs WLP810 San Francisco Lager

Original gravity: 1.091 (21.8°P)
Final gravity: 1.024 (6.1°P)
ABV: 8.8%
IBU: 37
SRM: 65

Directions

Prepare yeast starter of at least 2 to 3 quarts (1.9 to 2.8L) four to five days before brewing. Mash at 152°F to 153°F (66.7°C to 67°C), using 20 quarts (19L) of water. Pitch yeast starter into cooled wort and ferment at 40°F to 45°F (4.4°C to 7.2°C) for seven to ten days. Carry out a diacetyl rest at around 65°F (18.3°C) for a minimum of 48 hours before maturing for three to four months.

Notes

A big beer, yet very balanced, and one to be quaffed slowly so that the caramel and licorice notes can be savored alongside its chocolate character. I'm not sure where I got the name; it sounds as though it should be the title of an Ingmar Bergman film, but I assure you there's no Swedish angst about the beer.

Lenin's Doom Porter

(extract plus steeped grains)

Ingredients

6.0 lb. (2.7 kg) pale malt syrup (10°L); 63.2%
2.0 lb. (910 g) pale DME (10°L); 21%
1.0 lb. (454 g) UK crystal malt (80°L); 10.5%
0.25 lb. (113 g) Weyermann CARAFA I malt (340°L); 2.6%
0.25 lb. (113 g) Fawcett pale chocolate malt (200°L); 2.6%
1.0 oz. (28 g) Target pellets, 9.0% AA (9 AAU, 60 min.)
White Labs WLP810 San Francisco Lager; SAFALE W-34/70 Lager

Original gravity: 1.068 (16.6°P)
Final gravity: 1.018 (4.4°P)
ABV: 6.6%
IBU: 33
SRM: 59

Directions

Prepare yeast starter of at least 2 to 3 quarts (1.9 to 2.8L) several days ahead of brew day. Place grains in a muslin bag and steep them in 4 quarts (4L) hot water at around 160°F (71.1°C), strain and rinse thoroughly, using two lots of 4 quarts (4L) hot water. Use wort as liquor for dissolving extract, top up with water to boil volume. Pitch yeast starter into cooled wort and ferment at 40°F to 45°F (4.4°C to 7.2°C) for seven to ten days. Carry out a diacetyl rest at around 65°F (18.3°C) for a minimum of forty-eight hours before maturing for three to four weeks.

Notes

A reasonably strong beer, but still subtle, with chocolate and caramel flavors in the ascendant. It may be named after a noted revolutionary, but it is certainly not revolting!

Black Chairman Porter

(extract plus partial mash)

Ingredients

6.0 lb. (2.7 kg) amber malt syrup (20°L); 48%
1.5 lb. (680 g) amber DME (20°L); 12.8%
2.0 lb. (910 g) US 2-row pale malt (2°L); 16%
1.0 lb. (454 g) Crisp brown malt (65°L); 8%
0.5 lb. (227 g) Briess Special Roast malt (63°L); 4%
1.0 lb. (454 g) Weyermann Melanoidin malt (27°L); 8%
0.5 lb. (227 g) Briess BlackPrinz® malt (500°L); 4%
1.4 oz. (40 g) Perle pellets, 8.0% AA (11.2 AAU, 60 min.)
Saflager S-23 Lager; Brewferm Lager

Original gravity: 1.080 (19.3°P)
Final gravity: 1.022 (5.6°P)
ABV: 7.7%
IBU: 42
SRM: 106

Directions

Prepare yeast starter of at least 2 to 3 quarts (1.9 to 2.8L) several days ahead of brew day. Place grains in a muslin bag and mash in 6 quarts (5.7L) of hot water at 150°F to 152°F (65.6°C to 66.7°C) for forty-five to sixty minutes. Strain and rinse thoroughly, using two lots of 6 quarts (5.7L) of hot water. Use wort as liquor for dissolving extract, top up with water to boil volume. Pitch yeast starter into cooled wort and ferment at 40°F to 45°F (4.4°C to 7.2°C) for seven to ten days. Carry out a diacetyl rest at around 65°F (18.3°C) for a minimum of forty-eight hours before maturing for three to four weeks.

Notes

A big mouthful here, with a lot of body and mouthfeel coming from the variety of specialty malts used, especially the extra lusciousness from the Melanoidin malt. The name is a pun on a certain imported Baltic porter.

DRY STOUTS

Pat O'Nine Tails

(all-grain)

Ingredients

6.75 lb. (3.1 kg) US 2-row pale malt (2°L); 73.8%
0.5 lb. (227 g) Simpson roasted barley (550°L); 5.5%
1.4 lb. (640 g) flaked barley (1.5°L); 15.3%
0.5 lb. (227 g) Crisp black malt (600°L); 5.5%
1.0 oz. (28 g) US Northern Brewer pellets, 9.0% AA (9 AAU, 90 min.)
Wyeast 1084 Irish Ale; White Labs WLP 004 Irish Ale

Original gravity: 1.043 (10.7°P)
Final gravity: 1.010 (2.6°P)
ABV: 4.1%
IBU: 34
SRM: 118

Directions

Mash at 148°F to 150°F (64.4°C to 65.6°C) with 11 quarts (11L) of hot water; mature two to three weeks.

Notes

A more or less classic Irish dry stout, with enough roast malt flavor to make it almost harsh. This one should definitely be served under nitrogen or mixed gas. The name suggests there may be something masochistic in liking a beer with this kind of bite?

Flakes Away Stout

(all-grain)

Ingredients

5.5 lb. (2.5 kg) Briess mild ale malt (5°L); 67.9%
0.8 lb. (360 g) Briess Victory malt (28°L); 9.9%
0.8 lb. (360 g) UK crystal malt (60°L); 9.9%
0.6 lb. (272 g) Baird chocolate malt (450°L); 7.4%
0.4 lb. (180 g) Baird black malt (550°L); 4.9%
0.7 oz. (20 g) Magnum pellets, 12.0% AA (8.4 AAU, 90 min.)
Wyeast 1335 British Ale II; White Labs WLP 023 Burton Ale

Original gravity: 1.038 (9.5°P)
Final gravity: 1.010 (2.6°P)
ABV: 3.6%
IBU: 31
SRM: 117

Directions

Mash at 150°F to 152°F (65.6°C to 66.7°C) using 10 quarts (9.5L) water; mature one to two weeks.

Notes

Here we move away from the classic version of this beer to a more balanced drink, yet still with a characteristic bite, but modified because of the small proportion of black malt in the grist. That is because this is intended as a session beer, small enough to have more than one. The derivation of the name is obvious; I took out the flakes because they have little flavor effect and would only have diluted the malt flavors in this light beer.

My Way Stout

(all-grain)

Ingredients

5.75 lb. (2.6 kg) UK mild ale malt (4°L); 56.1%
1.0 lb. (454 g) Briess Munich malt (10°L); 9.8%
1.0 lb. (454 g) Belgian Vienna malt (4°L); 9.8%
1.0 lb. (454 g) Weyermann Melanoidin malt (27°L); 9.8%
1.0 lb. (454 g) Crisp brown malt (65°L); 9.8%
0.25 lb. (113 g) Belgian Special B malt (140°L); 2.4%
0.25 lb. (113 g) Briess BlackPrinz® malt (500°L); 2.4%
1.75 oz. (50 g) UK First Gold pellets, 6.5% AA (11.4 AAU, 90 min.)
Wyeast 1187 RingwoodAle; White Labs WLP 004 Irish Ale

Original gravity: 1.048 (11.9°P)
Final gravity: 1.013 (3.3°P)
ABV: 4.5%
IBU: 43
SRM: 58

Directions

Mash at 150°F (65.6°C) with 13 quarts (12L) water; mature one to two weeks.

Notes

Though this is still a dry stout, and still a session beer, I have edged away from the austere character of the original to produce a beer with a lot more depth behind the roast malt taste, and the roast character is muted by the use of de-bittered black malt. The name refers to me, not to Sinatra; I doubt he drank dry stout!

New World Irish Stout

(extract plus steeped grains)

Ingredients

4.0 lb. (1.8 kg) amber malt syrup (20°L); 72.1%
0.8 lb. (360 g) amber DME (20°L); 14.4%
0.5 lb. (227 g) Weyermann CARAFA III malt (520°L); 9%
0.25 lb. (113 g) Paul's black malt (550°L); 4.5%
1.8 oz. (51 g) US Goldings pellets, 4.5% AA (8 AAU, 60 min.)
Wyeast 1084 Irish Ale; Danstar Windsor Ale

Original gravity: 1.039 (10.8°P)
Final gravity: 1.010 (2.6°P)
ABV: 3.7%
IBU: 30
SRM: 99

Directions

Place grains in a muslin bag and steep them in 1 quart (1L) hot water at around 160°F (71.1°C), strain and rinse thoroughly, using two lots of 1 quart (1L) hot water. Use wort as liquor for dissolving extract, top up with water to boil volume. Mature one to two weeks.

Notes

This first extract recipe for this style is similar to the Irish original, with an almost one-dimensional roasted character, partly because it is meant to be simple to brew, and simple to drink. I called it New World Stout because I had just been listening to Dvorak's symphony of the same name.

Special Smoothie Stout

(extract plus steeped grains)

Ingredients

6.0 lb. (2.7 kg) pale malt syrup (10°L); 80%
0.5 lb. (227 g) Briess caramel malt (40°L); 6.7%
0.25 lb. (113 g) Belgian Special B malt (140°L); 3.3%
0.25 lb. (113 g) Fawcett pale chocolate malt (200°L); 3.3%
0.25 lb. (113 g) Crisp roasted barley (530°L); 3.3%
0.25 lb. (113 g) Briess BlackPrinz® malt (500°L); 3.3%
2.75 oz. (78 g) Fuggles pellets, 4.0% AA (11 AAU, 60 min.)
Munton's Ale; Danstar Nottingham Ale

Original gravity: 1.050 (12.4°P)
Final gravity: 1.013 (3.3°P)
ABV: 4.8%
IBU: 41
SRM: 85

Directions

Place grains in a muslin bag and steep them in 2 quarts (1.9L) hot water at around 160°F (71.1°C), strain and rinse thoroughly, using two lots of 2 quarts (1.9L) hot water. Use wort as liquor for dissolving extract, top up with water to boil volume. Mature two to three weeks.

Notes

This is a much more complicated dry stout and exhibits a wide spectrum of flavors beyond the burnt tastes of the two high-roasted malts, with chocolate, raisin, and caramel flavors battling the roasted malts to give a more balanced beer than is usual for this style. The derivation of this name might appear to be obvious, but is really a reference to a British slang name for a persuasive talker who turns you to his will before you realize what has happened. And this beer, still at a "session" level of 4.8% abv, can do just that!

Wilde Variety Stout

(extract plus partial mash)

Ingredients

4.0 lb. (1.8 kg) amber malt syrup (20°L); 48.5%
2.0 lb. (910 g) US 2-row pale malt (2°L); 24.2%
0.5 lb. (227 g) Briess Special Roast malt (63°L); 6.1%
0.5 lb. (227 g) Baird brown malt (58°L); 6.1%
0.5 lb. (227 g) Crisp amber malt (29°L); 6.1%
0.5 lb. (227 g) Briess dark chocolate malt (420°L); 6.1%
0.25 lb. (113 g) Briess Black Barley (500°L); 3%
1.0 oz. (28 g) Nugget pellets, 10.0% AA (10 AAU, 60 min.)
Wyeast 1187 Ringwood Ale; White Labs 023 Burton Ale

Original gravity: 1.046 (11.4°P)
Final gravity: 1.011 (2.8°P)
ABV: 4.5%
IBU: 37
SRM: 99

Directions

Place grains in a muslin bag and mash in 5 quarts (4.7L) of hot water at 150°F to 152°F (65.6°C to 66.7°C) for forty-five to sixty minutes. Strain and rinse thoroughly, using two lots of 5 quarts (4.7L) of hot water. Use wort as liquor for dissolving extract, top up with water to boil volume. Mature one to three weeks.

Notes

This is a very drinkable beer, but with lots of different flavors (chocolate, roast, nutty, dried fruit, licorice) creeping over your palate as you savor it. I admit it is quite a big partial mash, but this will be justified by the beer having plenty of flavor while still at a very comfortable 4.5% abv. Remember that if you use the Ringwood yeast, you should control the fermentation temperature at ± 65°F (18°C) as closely as you can, so that you don't get too much diacetyl in the beer. I went "Wilde" on the malts as a nod to Ireland's famous writer and wit.

A favorite Denver, Colorado, watering hole.

SWEET STOUTS

Milkmaid's Best Stout

(all-grain)

Ingredients
6.5 lb. (2.95 kg) US 2-row pale malt (2°L); 69.5%
0.5 lb. (227 g) Briess Special Roast malt (63°L); 5.4%

0.75 lb. (340 g) Briess caramel malt (80°L); 8%
0.25 lb. (113 g) Crisp chocolate malt (450°L); 2.7%
0.25 lb. (113 g) Munton's black malt (450°L); 2.7%
0.1 lb. (45 g) Munton's roasted barley (550°L); 1.1%
1.0 lb. (454 g) lactose; 10.7%
1.5 oz. (43 g) Glacier pellets, 5.0% AA (7.5 AAU, 90 min.)
Wyeast 1968 London ESB; White Labs 013 London Ale

Original gravity: 1.049 (12.2°P)
Final gravity: 1.020 (5.1°P)
ABV: 3.7%
IBU: 28
SRM: 77

Directions
Mash at 152 to 154°F (66.7 to 67.8°C) with 10 quarts (9.5L) water; add lactose for last ten minutes of the wort boil; mature one to three weeks.

Notes
The varied contributions of the four specialty malts plus roasted barley ensure that there is much more to this beer than just cloying sweetness! Obviously, at 3.7% abv, you can drink this 'til the cows come home. No prizes for how I came up with the name.

Cream Cracker Stout

(all-grain)

Ingredients
4.5 lb. (2.0 kg) US 2-row pale malt (2°L); 34.6%
3.0 lb. (1.4 kg) Briess Munich malt (10°L); 23.1%
1.0 lb. (454 g) Briess caramel malt (60°L); 7.7%
2.0 lb. (910 g) Crisp brown malt (65°L); 15.4%

2.0 lb. (910 g) Weyermann Melanoidin malt (27°L); 15.4%
0.5 lb. (227 g) lactose; 3.9%
2.0 oz. (57 g) East Kent Goldings pellets, 4.5% AA (9 AAU, 90 min.)
Wyeast 1318 London Ale III; White Labs WLP 028 Edinburgh Ale

Original gravity: 1.065 (15.9°P)
Final gravity: 1.020 (5.1°P)
ABV: 5.9%
IBU: 34
SRM: 57

Directions
Mash at 150°F (65.6°C) with 16 quarts (15L) water; add lactose for last ten minutes of the wort boil; mature two to four weeks.

Notes
At first this might seem to use an unusually small proportion of base malt, but the Munich malt will help out with starch-degrading enzymes, and the low mash temperature should ensure good conversion of the Melanoidin and brown malts. The lactose and the Melanoidin and caramel malts combine to give a full and sweet beer, very chewy, yet still with interesting notes from the Munich and brown malts behind the sweetness. The name comes from an English cracker that is not sweet and does not have any cream in it, so go figure why I used it!

Couldn't Be Simpler
(extract only)

Ingredients
6.0 lb. (2.7 kg) Dark malt syrup (100°L); 85.7%
1.0 lb. (454 g) lactose; 14.3%
1.25 oz. (35 g) US Fuggles pellets, 5.0% AA (6.3 AAU, 60 min.)
Safale US-05; Danstar Windsor Ale

Original gravity: 1.054 (13.3°P)
Final gravity: 1.022 (5.6°P)
ABV: 4.1%
IBU: 23
SRM: 120

Directions

Dissolve syrup in 3 gallons (11L) hot water, and add water to bring to boil volume; add lactose for last ten minutes of the wort boil; mature one to three weeks.

Notes

A classic sweet stout with dominant sweetness, this is very easy to brew, and still enjoyable to drink—and has the virtue of being quite low in alcohol. If you find it too simple, try adding a couple of cups of freshly brewed espresso coffee as you rack from the primary to secondary fermenter. I'm having difficulty remembering why I gave it such a name.

Cream of the Crop Stout

(extract plus partial mash)

Ingredients

6.0 lb. (2.7 kg) pale malt syrup (10°L); 64.9%
0.25 lb. (113 g) pale DME (10°L); 2.7%
1.0 lb. (454 g) US 2-row pale malt (2°L); 10.8%
0.5 lb. (227 g) Crisp brown malt (65°L); 5.4%
0.5 lb. (227 g) Briess caramel malt (120°L); 5.4%
0.25 lb. (113 g) Belgian Special B malt (140°L); 2.7%
0.25 lb. (113 g) Simpson roasted barley (550°L); 2.7%
0.5 lb. (227 g) lactose (5.4%)
1.4 oz. (40 g) Mt. Hood pellets, 6.0% AA (8.4 AAU, 60 min.)
Wyeast 1098 British Ale; White Labs WLP 013 London Ale

Original gravity: 1.062 (15.2°P)
Final gravity: 1.020 (5.1°P)

ABV: 5.5%
IBU: 32
SRM: 66

Directions

Place grains in a muslin bag and mash at 148°F (64.4°C) with 3 quarts (2.8L) water for forty-five minutes to one hour. Rinse grains with two lots of 3 quarts (2.8L) hot water and use collected wort to dissolve extracts; make to boil volume with water. Add lactose for last ten minutes of the wort boil; mature two to four weeks.

Notes

In this beer, the lactose has been reduced, and the grains mashed at relatively low temperatures in order to lower the level of sweetness. There is a multitude of different flavors from the use of specialty malts, which further makes this beer more about the malts than about lactose sweetness, although it is still luscious enough to fit into the sweet stout category. It is harder to brew than the previous extract version, yet much more enjoyable to drink, in my opinion. And the name? I had to call it something, didn't I?

FOREIGN EXTRA STOUTS

Old Sternface Stout

(all-grain)

Ingredients

12.0 lb. (5.4 kg) Briess Ashburne® mild ale malt (5°L); 80%
1.5 lb. (680 g) UK crystal malt (40°L); 10%
0.5 lb. (227 g) Fawcett black malt (450°L); 3.3%
1.0 lb. (454 g) Briess Roasted Barley (300°L); 6.7%
1.3 oz. (37 g) Magnum pellets, 14.0% AA (18 AAU, 90 min.)
Wyeast 1084 Irish Ale; White Labs WLP 004 Irish Ale

Original gravity: 1.071 (17.3°P)
Final gravity: 1.018 (4.6°P)

ABV: 6.9%
IBU: 67
SRM: 129

Directions

Mash at 150 to 152°F (65.6 to 66.7°C) with 19 quarts (18L) of water; mature three to six weeks.

Notes

I have tried to keep the harshness down a little by using a relatively light form of roasted barley, but this is an unforgiving beer—little more than a stronger version of the dry stout style, which is what it was originally. Except, of course, that it does not have any of the slight sourness of the original Foreign Stout, nowadays achieved by Guinness through use of a "secret" extract. You could do the same by making another version of this beer (without the hops), pitching it with *Brettanomyces* yeast, and adding a portion of this to the above recipe. I haven't done this myself, so I can't give details of the procedure, but I would have thought adding about 2 percent (1 pint, 0.5L) of the soured beer to five gallons (19L) of the stout would be sufficient, and would be a small enough volume that you might even consider pasteurizing it yourself!

The name is self-explanatory, this beer takes no prisoners, for it has both bitterness and a roasted bite.

Hurricane in Kingston

(all-grain)

Ingredients

8.5 lb. (3.9 kg) US 2-row pale malt (2°L); 53.1%
3.0 lb. (1.4 kg) Briess Munich malt (10°L); 18.8%
2.0 lb. (910 g) Weyermann Melanoidin malt (27°L); 12.5%
0.5 lb. (227 g) Belgian Special B malt (140°L); 3.1%
1.0 lb. (454 g) Briess BlackPrinz® malt (500°L); 6.3%

1.0 lb. (454 g) Briess Roasted Barley (300°L); 6.3%
2.4 oz. (68 g) Brewer's Gold pellets, 9.0% AA (21.6 AAU, 90 min.)
Wyeast 1028 London Ale; Safale S-04 Ale

Original gravity: 1.076 (18.4°P)
Final gravity: 1.020 (5.1°P)
ABV: 7.3%
IBU: 81
SRM: 194

Directions
Mash at 152 to 154°F (66.7 to 67.8°C) with 20 quarts (19L) of water; mature three to six weeks.

Notes
A softer version of the style than the previous brew, this beer still has plenty of roasted coffee flavors, but the harshness of the roasted malts is balanced by the full body due to the use of Munich and Melanoidin malts. Of course, just like Old Sternface, there is a significant amount of hop bitterness in this beer as well. The name arises from the time when I was stranded in a hotel in Kingston, Jamaica, and could do nothing but ride out the storm and drink Guinness Foreign Stout (which at that time was brewed on the island in Guinness's own Jamaican brewery).

No More Mr. Nice Guy Stout
(all-grain)

Ingredients
6.0 lb. (2.7 kg) UK mild ale malt (4°L); 38.1%
3.0 lb. (1.4 kg) Briess Munich malt (10°L); 19%
2.0 lb. (910 g) Briess Victory malt (28°L); 12.7%
1.5 lb. (680 g) UK crystal malt (80°L); 9.5%

1.0 lb. (454 g) Briess Special Roast malt (63°L); 6.3%
1.5 lb. (680 g) Briess BlackPrinz® malt (500°L); 9.5%
0.75 lb. (340 g) Weyermann Acidulated malt (1.8°L); 4.8%
1.5 oz. (43 g) Columbus pellets, 11.0% AA (16.5% AAU, 90 min.)
Wyeast 1056 American Ale; White Labs WLP 041 Pacific Ale

Original gravity: 1.074 (18.0°P)
Final gravity: 1.019 (4.8°P)
ABV: 7.2%
IBU: 62
SRM: 224

Directions
Mash at 152 to 154°F (66.7 to 67.8°C) using 20 quarts (19L) water; mature three to six weeks.

Notes
This recipe will produce something resembling the Dublin original, with some tartness from the acidulated malt, yet with a full-bodied character due to the several specialty malts used. Note that at first glance, the grain bill seems light on base malts, but the specialty malts mainly require only leaching, rather than mashing, so wort fermentability will not be a problem. The deliberate souring with acidulated malt is the source of the name.

Carib Delight

(extract plus steeped grains)

Ingredients
6.0 lb. (2.7 kg) amber malt syrup (20°L); 64.9%
1.75 lb. (790 g) amber DME (20°L); 18.9%
0.5 lb. (227 g) Belgian Special B malt (140°L); 5.4%
0.5 lb. (227 g) Dingeman's de-bittered black malt (550°L); 5.4%
0.5 lb. (227 g) Baird roasted barley (550°L); 5.4%

1.0 oz. (28 g) Admiral pellets, 14.0% AA (14 AAU, 60 min.)
Wyeast 1084 Irish Ale; White Labs WLP 004 Irish Ale

Original gravity: 1.066 (16.1°P)
Final gravity: 1.017 (4.3°P)
ABV: 6.4%
IBU: 52
SRM: 155

Directions

Place grains in a muslin bag and steep them in 2 quarts (1.9L) hot water at around 160°F (71.1°C), strain and rinse thoroughly, using two lots of 2 quarts (1.9L) hot water. Use wort as liquor for dissolving extract, top up with water to boil volume. Mature three to six weeks.

Notes

A fairly simple example of the style, largely dominated by roasted flavors but with a little extra character added by the Special B malt. However, I have muted the roasted flavors somewhat by using a de-bittered black malt. The name indicates the surprising fact that such beers should enjoy some popularity in a tropical climate.

Perfidious Albion Stout

(extract plus partial mash)

Ingredients

8.0 lb. (3.6 kg) Briess CBW Porter syrup (20°L); 64%
1.5 lb. (680 g) US 2-row pale malt (2°L); 12%
1.0 lb. (454 g) Briess Munich malt (10°L); 8%
1.0 lb. (454 g) Baird brown malt (58°L); 8%
1.0 lb. (454 g) Munton roasted barley (550°L); 8%
3.0 oz. (85 g) Bullion pellets, 7.0% AA (21 AAU, 60 min.)
Wyeast 1728 Scottish Ale; White Labs WLP 028 Edinburgh Ale

Original gravity: 1.078 (18.9°P)
Final gravity: 1.019 (4.8°P)
ABV: 7.8%
IBU: 52
SRM: 156

Directions

Place grains in a muslin bag and mash at 148°F (64.4°C) with 6 quarts (5.7L) water for forty-five minutes to one hour. Rinse grains with two lots of 6 quarts (5.7L) hot water and use collected wort to dissolve extracts; make to boil volume with water. Mature three to six weeks.

Notes

A version with more mouthfeel than the previous beer, with roasted notes more in the background, but with a little more alcohol to lead you astray. This is an Irish beer betrayed by perfidious albion (a.k.a. Britain)!

Leprechaun Tart

(extract plus partial mash)

Ingredients

7.0 lb. (3.2 kg) Munton pale malt syrup (10°L); 63.6%
1.5 lb. (680 g) US 2-row pale malt (2°L); 13.6%
0.5 lb. (227 g) Weyermann Melanoidin malt (27°L); 4.6%
1.0 lb. (454 g) Crisp brown malt (65°L); 9.1%
0.5 lb. (227 g) Munton black malt (450°L); 4.6%
0.5 lb. (227 g) Weyermann Acidulated malt (1.8°L); 4.6%
1.5 oz. (43 g) Chinook pellets, 11.0% AA (16.5 AAU, 60 min.)
Wyeast 1056 American Ale; Cooper's Ale

Original gravity: 1.069 (16.8°P)
Final gravity: 1.018 (4.6°P)

ABV: 6.7%
IBU: 62
SRM: 75

Directions

Place grains in a muslin bag and mash at 150°F (65.6°C) with 5 quarts (4.7L) water for forty-five minutes to one hour. Rinse grains with two lots of 5 quarts (4.7L) hot water and use collected wort to dissolve extracts; make to boil volume with water. Mature three to six weeks.

Notes

A companion to the all-grain attempt to match the Dublin original, with the tartness from the acidulated malt somewhat modified with a little sweetness from the Melanoidin malt. I do not know what kind of dish leprechaun tart may be, or whether you get three wishes after eating it, but at least this beer is good and refreshing!

OATMEAL STOUTS

St. Andrew's Pleasure

(all-grain)

Ingredients

7.5 lb. (3.4 kg) Maris Otter pale ale malt (4°L); 71.4%
1.0 lb. (454 g) UK crystal malt (80°L); 9.5%
1.0 lb. (454 g) Fawcett oat malt (3°L); 9.5%
0.5 lb. (227 g) Briess BlackPrinz® malt (500°L); 4.8%
0.5 lb. (227 g) Paul's chocolate malt (450°L); 4.8%
1.5 oz. (43 g) WGV pellets, 5.5% AA (8.3 AAU, 90 min.)
Wyeast 1968 London ESB; White Labs WLP 013 London Ale

Original gravity: 1.049 (12.2°P)
Final gravity: 1.012 (3.1°P)

ABV: 4.8%
IBU: 31
SRM: 118

Directions

Mash at 152 to 154°F (66.7 to 67.8°C) with 13 quarts (12L) of water; mature two to three weeks.

Notes

The use of de-bittered black malt and low-roasted chocolate malt allows the oats' silkiness to come through and deliver a well-balanced and easy-drinking smooth beer. At only 4.8% abv, it is also easy to drink it throughout a session. The name is simply a nod to the Scots who first came up with this style.

Easy Ryder

(all-grain)

Ingredients

4.0 lb. (1.8 kg) UK mild ale malt (4°L); 32.7%
0.5 lb. (227 g) Fawcett oat malt (3°L); 4.1%
2.0 lb. (910 g) Belgian Vienna malt (4°L); 16.3%
2.0 lb. (910 g) Briess Munich malt (10°L); 16.3%
2.0 lb. (910 g) Weyermann Melanoidin malt (27°L); 16.3%
1.0 lb. (454 g) Briess Special Roast malt (63°L); 8.2%
0.75 lb. (340 g) Simpson chocolate malt (410°L); 6.1%
1.25 oz. (34 g) Centennial pellets, 8.5% AA (10.6 AAU, 90 min.)
Wyeast 1099 Whitbread Ale; White Labs WLP002 English Ale

Original gravity: 1.058 (14.3°P)
Final gravity: 1.016 (4.1°P)
ABV: 5.5%

IBU: 40
SRM: 94

Directions

Mash at 150°F (65.6°C) with 15 quarts (14L) of water; mature two to three weeks.

Notes

In this instance, the beer is brewed with a relatively low proportion of high-roasted malt, which, along with the addition of Melanoidin and the other specialty malts, results in a smoothly mellow drink that is a tad too high in alcohol to be a true session beer. In case you are not sure about the low proportion of the base mild ale malt, remember that the Munich and Vienna malts both contain enzymes, and between the three malts there should be no problem with starch conversion. The name refers to the prestigious team competition in golf, the Ryder Cup, which is another nod to Scotland, the home of golf.

Hammertonian Equation

(all-grain)

Ingredients

4.0 lb. (1.8 kg)UK mild ale malt (4°L); 37.2%
1.0 lb. (454 g) Briess oat flakes (2.5°L); 9.3%
1.0 lb. (454 g) Weyermann rye malt (3°L); 9.3%
2.0 lb. (910 g) Crisp brown malt (65°L); 18.6%
1.0 lb. (454 g) Crisp amber malt (29°L); 9.3%
1.0 lb. (454 g) Briess Victory malt (28°L); 9.3%
0.5 lb. (227 g) Belgian Special B malt (140°L); 4.7%
0.25 lb. (113 g) Briess BlackPrinz® malt (500°L); 2.3%
1.0 oz. (28 g) Northdown pellets, 7.5% AA (7.5 AAU, 90 min.)
Wyeast 1028 London Ale; White Labs WLP013 English Ale

Original gravity: 1.051 (12.6°P)
Final gravity: 1.013 (3.3°P)
ABV: 4.9%
IBU: 28
SRM: 81

Directions

Mash at 148 to 150°F (64.4 to 65.6°C) with 13 quarts (12L) of water; mature one to three weeks.

Notes

Use of only a small proportion of de-bittered black malt backed up by a riot of specialty malts melds into a full-bodied but very drinkable session beer. The quite low proportion of base malt should be able to handle the main starch-containing specialty malts, brown and amber, but I went for a low-end mash temperature to maximize conversion. The name is a pun on "Hammerton," one-time brewers of oatmeal stout in the area of South London where I lived in the 1950s and

A new brewery in Stratford, Connecticut.

1960s, and on the famed "Hamiltonian equation," an important part of the mathematics of quantum theory.

Healthy Breakfast Stout

(extract plus partial mash)

Ingredients

4.0 lb. (1.8 kg) Munton's light malt syrup (10°L); 51.6%
1.5 lb. (680 g) US 2-row pale malt (2°L); 19.4%
0.5 lb. (227 g) Briess oat flakes (2.5°L); 6.5%
0.75 lb. (340 g) UK crystal malt (120°L); 9.7%
0.5 lb. (227 g) Belgian Special B malt (140°L); 6.5%
0.5 lb. (227 g) Baird chocolate malt (450°L); 6.5%
1.75 oz. (50 g) UK Fuggles pellets, 4.0% AA (7 AAU, 60 min.)
Safale S-04 Ale; Munton's Ale

Original gravity: 1.046 (11.4°P)
Final gravity: 1.014 (3.6°P)
ABV: 4.1%
IBU: 26
SRM: 86

Directions

Place grains in a muslin bag and mash at 150 to 152°F (65.6 to 66.7°C) with 5 quarts (4.7L) water for forty-five minutes to one hour. Rinse grains with two lots of 5 quarts (4.7L) hot water and use collected wort to dissolve extracts; make to boil volume with water; mature one to two weeks.

Notes

Chocolate is the only high-roast malt in this brew, and it comes in only slightly so that the beer turns out as a silky but chewy and relatively low gravity beer that satisfies the palate without overdoing the alcohol.

The name? Well, you do have oats for breakfast, don't you? They are supposed to be good for you.

Corked Cask Stout

(extract plus partial mash)

Ingredients

6.0 lb. (2.7 kg) amber malt syrup (20°L); 63.2%
2.0 lb. (910 g) US 2-row pale malt (2°L); 21.1%
0.5 lb. (227 g) Briess oat flakes (2.5°L); 5.3%
0.5 lb. (227 g) Weyermann Melanoidin malt (27°L); 5.3%
0.5 lb. (227 g) Crisp black malt (600°L); 5.3%
2.0 oz. (57 g) Willamette pellets, 5.0% AA (10 AAU, 60 min.)
Wyeast 1084 Irish Ale; White Labs WLP004 Irish Ale

Original gravity: 1.060 (14.7°P)
Final gravity: 1.016 (4.1°P)
ABV: 5.7%
IBU: 37
SRM: 88

Directions

Place grains in a muslin bag and mash at 151 to 153°F (66.1 to 67.2°C) with 4.5 quarts (4.3L) water for forty-five minutes to one hour. Rinse grains with two lots of 5 quarts (4.7L) hot water and use collected wort to dissolve extracts; make to boil volume with water; mature two to four weeks.

Notes

A somewhat simple recipe, but a lusciously smooth beer held back from sweetness by the bite of black malt. A little high in alcohol, it is not quite a session beer. The name is just a bit of thumbing my nose at wine aficionados.

Vicar's Tipple

(extract plus partial mash)

Ingredients

4.5 lb. (2.0 kg) Briess CBW porter syrup (20°L); 50%
2.0 lb. (910 g) US 2-row pale malt (2°L); 22.2%
0.5 lb. (227 g) Briess oat flakes (2.5°L); 5.6%
0.5 lb. (227 g) Briess caramel malt (20°L); 5.6%
0.5 lb. (227 g) Briess caramel malt (80°L); 5.6%
0.5 lb. (227 g) Belgian Special B malt (140°L); 5.6%
0.5 lb. (227 g) Fawcett chocolate malt (360°L); 5.6%
1.2 oz. (34 g) First Gold pellets, 7.0% AA (60 min.)
Wyeast 1099 Whitbread Ale; White Labs WLP013 London Ale

Original gravity: 1.053 (13.1°P)
Final gravity: 1.013 (3.3°P)
ABV: 5.2%
IBU: 31
SRM: 79

Directions

Place grains in a muslin bag and mash at 151 to 153°F (66.1 to 67.2°C) with 6 quarts (5.7L) water for forty-five minutes to one hour. Rinse grains with two lots of 6 quarts (5.7L) hot water and use collected wort to dissolve extracts; make to boil volume with water; mature two to three weeks.

Notes

In this brew, the caramel malts and Special B give a touch of sweetness, as well as caramel and raisin notes to round out the silkiness of the oats, all of which is balanced by the muted roast character of the chocolate malt. With a fairly modest alcohol content, you might well allow yourself a second or even third glass of this beauty. Where does the name come from? How should I know, I only write this stuff!

AMERICAN STOUTS

Strike One!

(all-grain)

Ingredients

8.0 lb. (3.6 kg) US 2-row pale malt (2°L); 53.3%
5.0 lb. (2.3 kg) Briess Munich malt (10°L); 33.3%
1.0 lb. (454 g) US caramel malt (40°L); 6.7%
0.5 lb. (227 g) Briess roasted barley (300°L); 3.3%
0.5 lb. (227 g) Weyermann CARAFA II malt (430°L); 3.3%
1.5 oz. (43 g) Chinook pellets, 12.0% AA (18 AAU, 90 min.)
1 oz. (28g) Cascade pellets, 6% AA (0 min.)
Wyeast 1056 American Ale; White Labs WLP001 California Ale

Original gravity: 1.071 (17.3°P)
Final gravity: 1.018 (4.6°P)
ABV: 6.9%
IBU: 67 (76 with late addition contribution)
SRM: 94

Directions

Mash at 150°F (65.6°C) with 19 quarts (18L) of water, add Chinook hops at start and Cascade at end of boil; mature three to five weeks.

Notes

This has a medium level of roast flavor, but, as you might expect, this is almost drowned out by the high bitterness and the Cascade hop character in the finish. The caramel and Munich malts add a little background sweetness and body, but it's all about the hops, as it should be. All the ingredients are American, so the name comes from the great American game of baseball (of course).

Seventh-Inning Stretch

(all-grain)

Ingredients

6.0 lb. (2.7 kg) US 2-row pale malt (2°L); 47.1%
2.0 lb. (910 g) Briess Munich malt (10°L); 15.7%
2.0 lb. (910 g) Belgian Vienna malt (4°L); 15.7%
1.0 lb. (454 g) Weyermann Melanoidin malt (27°L); 7.8%
0.5 lb. (227 g) Belgian Biscuit malt (25°L); 3.9%
0.75 lb. (340 g) Briess Special Roast malt (63°L); 5.9%
0.5 lb. (227 g) Briess BlackPrinz® malt (500°L); 3.9%
1.0 oz. (28 g) Tomahawk pellets, 16.0% AA (16 AAU; 90 min.)
1 oz. (28 g) Crystal pellets, 3% AA (20 min.)
0.5 oz. (14g g) Citra pellets, 11% AA (0 min.)
Wyeast 1272 American Ale II; White Labs WLP008 East Coast Ale

Original gravity: 1.060 (14.7°P)
Final gravity: 1.018 (4.6°P)
ABV: 5.5%
IBU: 60 (73 with late addition contribution)
SRM: 75

Directions

Mash at 149 to 151°F (65.0 to 66.1°C) with 16 quarts (15L) of water; add Tomahawk hops at start of boil, Crystal hops for last twenty minutes, and Citra at end of boil; mature two to four weeks.

Notes

The specialty malts provide a number of different flavors, while layered on top are the floral notes from the Crystal hop and the definite citrus flavor from Citra. I included Munich, Vienna, Melanoidin, biscuit, and Special B malts to add caramel, nutty, bready, and biscuity (graham cracker?) flavors so that the beer is balanced and not completely dominated by the hop bitterness and flavor. And, naturally, this also has to have a baseball-derived name, but why don't they have halftime in baseball as they do in football?

Out of the Park

(all-grain)

Ingredients

5.0 lb. (2.27 kg) Briess Ashburne® mild ale malt (5°L); 43.5%
1.0 lb. (454 g) US caramel malt (20°L); 8.7%
1.5 lb. (680 g) Briess Victory malt (28°L); 13%
3.0 lb. (1.36 kg) Crisp brown malt (65°L); 26.1%
0.5 lb. (227 g) Fawcett pale chocolate malt (200°L); 4.4%
0.5 lb. (227 g) Briess roasted barley (300°L); 4.4%
1.1 oz. (31 g) Simcoe pellets, 13.0% AA (14.3 AAU, 90 min.)
0.5 oz. (14 g) Cascade pellets, 6% AA (10 min.)
0.5 oz. (14 g) Mt. Hood pellets, 5% AA (0 min.)
Nottingham Ale; White Labs WLP060 American Ale Blend

Original gravity: 1.054 (13.3°P)
Final gravity: 1.013 (3.3°P)
ABV: 5.3%
IBU: 53 (61 with late addition contribution)
SRM: 106

Directions

Mash at 150 to 151°F (65.6 to 66.1°C) with 14 quarts (13L) of water; add Simcoe at start of boil, Cascade for last ten minutes, and Mt. Hood at end of boil; mature two to four weeks.

Notes

The combination of malts, starting with mild ale, and through low- to high-roasted malts is enough to convince you that this is a stout, yet the mix of hop flavors leaves you in no doubt that it is an American stout. With extra bitterness from the late hop additions, this reaches a relatively high level of IBU for a 5.3% abv beer, but the malts are enough to balance this. I like this one a lot—in fact, as you see from the name, I think it's a home run!

Easy Does It

(extract plus steeped grains)

Ingredients

6.0 lb. (2.7 kg) Munton dark malt syrup (60°L); 64.9%
1.25 lb. (567 g) Munton dark DME (20°L); 13.5%
1.0 lb. (454 g) UK crystal malt (60°L); 10.8%
0.5 lb. (227 g) Belgian Special B malt (140°L); 5.4%
0.5 lb. (227 g) Baird chocolate malt (450°L); 5.4%
1.75 oz. (50 g) Galena pellets, 10.0% AA (17.5 AAU, 60 min.)
0.5 oz. (14 g) Cascade pellets, 6% AA (0 min.)
0.5 oz. (14 g) Columbus pellets, 14% AA (0 min.)
Wyeast 1056 American Ale; White Labs 001 California Ale

Original gravity: 1.063 (15.4°P)
Final gravity: 1.016 (4.1°P)
ABV: 6.2%
IBU: 66 (81 with contribution from late addition)
SRM: 148

Directions

Place grains in a muslin bag and steep them in 3 quarts (2.8L) hot water at around 160°F (71.1°C), strain and rinse thoroughly, using two lots of 3 quarts (2.8L) hot water. Use wort as liquor for dissolving extract, top up with water to boil. Add Galena hops at start of boil, Cascade and Columbus hops at end of boil; mature three to four weeks.

Notes

Here we go again, with the flavors of a relatively simple mix of malts underpinned with the grapefruit taste from Cascade and the somewhat earthy flavor of Columbus hops. If you get all the bitterness from the late hop addition, you may well wonder just what is the difference between a so-called black IPA and an American stout. The name of this beer is obvious; I ran out of baseball metaphors!

Don't Tailgate Me!

(extract plus steeped grains)

Ingredients

8.0 lb. (3.63 kg) Munton's amber malt syrup (30°L); 71.1%
0.75 lb. (340 g) Munton's light DME (12°L); 6.7%
1.0 lb. (454 g) Weyermann CARARYE crystal rye malt (65°L); 8.9%
1.0 lb. (454 g) Belgian Special B malt (140°L); 8.9%
0.5 lb. (227 g) Dingeman's chocolate malt (340°L); 4.4%
3.0 oz. (85 g) Cluster pellets, 7.0% AA (21 AAU, 60 min.)
0.5 oz. (14 g) Chinook pellets 12% AA (5 min.)
0.5 oz. (14 g) Cascade pellets 6% AA (0 min.)
0.5 oz. (14 g) Horizon pellets 11% AA (0 min.)
Wyeast 1332 Northwest Ale; White Labs WLP051 California V

Original gravity: 1.075 (18.2°P)
Final gravity: 1.020 (5.1°P)
ABV: 7.2%
IBU: 78 (99 with contribution from late addition)
SRM: 125

Directions

Place grains in a muslin bag and steep them in 3 quarts (2.8L) hot water at around 160°F (71.1°C), strain and rinse thoroughly, using two lots of 3 quarts (2.8L) hot water. Use wort as liquor for dissolving extract, top up with water to boil volume. Add Cluster hops at start of boil, Chinook five minutes before end, and Cascade and Horizon hops at end of boil; mature three to five weeks.

Notes

The IBU level is a calculated figure and will probably not be this high in reality, though this beer will give any double IPA a run for its money! Once more, this quite big beer is notable for its floral/citrus/piney characters from Horizon/Cascade/Chinook that are amplified by the spicy character from the crystal rye malt. The name comes from the fact that this is a distinctive beer that will not be pushed around by anybody.

Three-Pointer

(extract plus partial mash)

Ingredients

5.0 lb. (2.27 kg) Munton's amber malt syrup (30°L); 52.6%
2.0 lb. (910 g) US 2-row pale malt (2°L); 21.1%
1.0 lb. (454 g) Crisp brown malt (65°L); 10.5%
0.5 lb. (227 g) Crisp amber malt (29°L); 5.3%
1.0 lb. (454 g) UK crystal malt (120°L); 10.5%
1.0 oz. (28 g) Magnum pellets, 14.0% AA (14 AAU, 60 min.)
1 oz. (28 g) Cascade pellets, 6% AA (10 min.)
0.5 oz. (14 g) Citra pellets, 12% AA (0 min.)
Wyeast 1272 American Ale II; White Labs WLP008 East
    Coast Ale

Original gravity: 1.057 (14.0°P)
Final gravity: 1.015 (3.8°P)
ABV: 5.5%
IBU: 52 (70 with contribution from late addition)
SRM: 71

Directions

Place grains in a muslin bag and mash at 150 to 152°F (65.6 to 66.7°C) with 6 quarts (5.7L) water for forty-five minutes to one hour. Rinse grains with two lots of 6 quarts (5.7L) hot water and use collected wort to dissolve extract; make to boil volume with water; add Magnum hops at start, Cascade hops for last ten minutes, and Citra hops at end of boil; mature two to four weeks.

Notes

Yes, it's all about the hops, with Cascade back again, but the very citrusy Citra lords it over the mix of malt flavors. If all the late addition contribution is realized, this beer will have a high bitterness for the alcohol content, but the specialty malts (brown/amber/crystal) will help to balance this. And the name comes from this brew being a winning shot on the buzzer!

Face-off of Jeff Browning and Rob Leonard and his team on Open Day during GABF at Great Divide brewery, Denver, Colorado.

IMPERIAL STOUTS

Nevsky Prospect

(all-grain)

Ingredients

8.5 lb. (3.86 kg) US 2-row pale malt (2°L); 44.7%
4.0 lb. (1.81 kg) Briess Munich malt (10°L); 21.1%
4.0 lb. (1.81 kg) Belgian Vienna malt (4°L); 21.1%
1.0 lb. (454 g) Briess Victory malt (28°L); 5.3%
0.5 lb. (227 g) Belgian Special B malt (140°L); 2.6%
0.5 lb. (227 g) Baird chocolate malt (450°L); 2.6%
0.5 lb. (227 g) Fawcett pale chocolate malt (200°L); 2.6%
2.5 oz. (71 g) Challenger pellets, 7.5% AA (19 AAU, 90 min.)
Wyeast 1056 American Ale; White Labs WLP007 Dry English Ale

Original gravity: 1.090 (21.5°P)
Final gravity: 1.025 (6.3°P)
ABV: 8.6%
IBU: 70
SRM: 99

Directions

Mash at 148 to 150°F (64.4 to 65.6°C) using 24 quarts (23L) of water; use a 2- to 3-quart (1.9 to 2.8L) yeast starter and mature four to six weeks.

Notes

A high gravity beer with lots of alcohol and a medley of malts to produce enough flavors to balance the alcohol, with perhaps a little emphasis on chocolate notes. Just to show that you really can get chocolate flavor without actually adding chocolate. The name had to be Russian, and for the record, the last time I walked down Nevsky Prospekt, it was in Leningrad, not St. Petersburg!

Big Brown Beast

(all-grain)

Ingredients

13.5 lb. (6.1 kg) Briess Ashburne® mild ale malt (5°L); 58.1%
6.0 lb. (2.7 kg) Briess Munich malt (10°L); 25.8%
1.0 lb. (454 g) Briess Special Roast malt (63°L); 4.3%
1.0 lb. (454 g) Belgian Biscuit malt (25°L); 4.3%
0.75 lb. (340 g) Weyermann CARAFA I malt (340°L); 3.2%
1.0 lb. (454 g) Simpson roasted barley (550°L); 4.3%
2.0 oz. 57 g) Nugget pellets, 11.5% AA (23 AAU, 90 min.)
Wyeast 1728 Scottish Ale; White Labs WLP028 Edinburgh Ale

Original gravity: 1.110 (25.8°P)
Final gravity: 1.030 (7.6°P)
ABV: 10.6%
IBU: 86
SRM: 204

Directions

Mash at 148 to 150°F (64.4 to 65.6°C) with 29 quarts (28L) of water; you may need to sparge and collect 7 gallons (27L) of wort and boil down to 5 gallons (19L) to get the target gravity. Use a big yeast starter, at least 3 quarts (2.8L), and mature for three to six months.

Notes

This is the strongest beer in this book, with a symphony of flavors (including bready and biscuity, as well as roasted notes) to match the high alcohol level. Achieving good attenuation is crucial with this brew, which might otherwise be overly sweet (which is why I used the low mash temperature to help dry out the beer). This beer is a good candidate for some added oak flavor (see how under the Porter and Stout

Raw Materials chapter). I am not sure that Russian bears are brown, but it seemed like an appropriate name.

Importerant Export

(all-grain)

Ingredients

8.0 lb. (3.63 kg) US 2-row pale malt (2°L); 47.1%
1.0 lb. (454 g) Weyermann rye malt (3°L); 5.9%
3.0 lb. (1.36 kg) Crisp brown malt (65°L); 17.7%
3.0 lb. (1.36 g) Crisp amber malt (29°L); 17.7%
1.0 lb. (454 g) Briess Victory malt (28°L); 5.9%
1.0 lb. (454 g) Dingeman De-bittered black malt (550°L); 5.9%
1.5 oz. (43 g) Columbus pellets, 11.0% AA (16.5 AAU, 90 min.)
Wyeast 1272 American Ale II; White Labs WLP060 American Ale
   Blend

Original gravity: 1.080 (19.3°P)
Final gravity: 1.022 (5.6°P)
ABV: 7.7%
IBU: 62
SRM: 176

Directions

Mash at 148 to 150°F (64.4 to 65.6°C) using 21 quarts (20L) of water; use a big yeast starter, at least 2 to 3 quarts (1.9 to 2.8L), and mature for three to six months.

Notes

This is a multi-flavored beer, with only muted roasted notes from the de-bittered black malt matched by the spicy edge of rye malt, the licorice from the brown malt, and biscuit and bready flavors from the amber and Victory malts. The name is just a silly play on words, what can I say?

Empressive Stout

(extract plus steeped grains)

Ingredients

8.0 lb. (3.63 kg) Munton's amber malt syrup (30°L); 58.2%
3.0 lb. (1.36 g) Munton's pale DME (12°L); 21.8%
1.0 lb. (454 g) Belgian Special B malt (140°L); 7.3%
1.0 lb. (454 g) Fawcett pale chocolate malt (200°L); 7.3%
0.75 lb. (340 g) Briess roasted barley (300°L); 5.5%
1.5 oz. (43 g) Millennium pellets, 14.0% AA (21 AAU, 60 min.)
Nottingham Ale; Safale S-33 Ale

Original gravity: 1.097 (23.0°P)
Final gravity: 1.030 (7.6°P)
ABV: 8.8%
IBU: 78
SRM: 168

Directions

Place grains in a muslin bag and steep them in 3 quarts (2.8L) hot water at around 160°F (71.1°C), strain and rinse thoroughly, using two lots of 3 quarts (2.8L) hot water. Use wort as liquor for dissolving extract, top up with water to boil volume. Use at least a 2- to 3-quart (1.9 to 2.8L) yeast starter and mature three to six months.

Notes

A straightforward beer to brew, yet still big in body and flavor, with the roasted barley providing a nice edge to balance the fullness derived from the other malts. The Nottingham yeast in particular tends to give good attenuation, so residual sweetness should not be a problem here.

The name is obvious, in that Russian stout was first exported from Britain to the court of Catherine the Great.

Whistlin' in the Dark

(extract plus partial mash)

Ingredients

8.0 lb. (3.63 kg) Briess pale malt syrup (10°L); 60.4%
0.75 lb. (340 g) Briess light DME (10°L); 5.7%
2.0 lb. (910 g) US 2-row pale malt (2°L); 15.1%
1.0 lb. (454 g) Crisp brown malt (65°L); 7.6%
0.5 lb. (227 g) Baird crystal rye malt (90°L); 3.8%
0.5 lb. (227 g) Briess BlackPrinz® malt (500°L); 3.8%
0.5 lb. (227 g) Munton's roasted barley (550°L); 3.8%
1.5 oz. (43 g) Horizon pellets, 12.0% AA (18 AAU, 60 min.)
Wyeast 1332 Northwest Ale; White Labs WLP013 London Ale

Original gravity: 1.085 (20.3°P)
Final gravity: 1.022 (5.6°P)
ABV: 8.3%
IBU: 67
SRM: 145

Directions

Place grains in a muslin bag and mash at 150 to152°F (65.6 to 66.7°C) with 6 quarts (5.7L) water for forty-five minutes to one hour. Rinse grains with two lots of 6 quarts (5.7L) hot water and use collected wort to dissolve extract; make to boil volume with water. Use a 2-quart (1.9L) yeast starter and mature two to four months.

Notes

This is a beer carrying a big punch from the black malt and roasted barley, which is offset by the licorice of the brown malt and the spiciness of the crystal rye malt. Whistling in the dark is supposed to keep the evil spirits at bay, but a glass of this beer will do that much better for you.

Ivan Idea

(extract plus partial mash)

Ingredients
8.0 lb. (3.63 kg) Munton's amber malt syrup (30°L); 64%
1.5 lb. (680 g) US 2-row pale malt (2°L); 12%
1.0 lb. (454 g) Briess Munich malt (10°L); 8%
1.0 lb. (454 g) Crisp amber malt (29°L); 8%
0.5 lb. (227 g) Briess Victory malt (28°L); 4%
0.5 lb. (227 g) Baird chocolate malt (450°L); 4%
1.5 oz. (43 g) US Northern Brewer pellets, 8.5% AA (12.8 AAU, 60 min.)
Wyeast 1275 Thames Valley Ale; White Labs WLP005 British Ale

Original gravity: 1.079 (19.1°P)
Final gravity: 1.020 (5.1°P)
ABV: 7.8%
IBU: 48
SRM: 104

Directions
Place grains in a muslin bag and mash at 151 to 153°F (66.1 to 67.2°C) with 6 quarts (5.7L) water for forty-five minutes to one hour. Rinse grains with two lots of 6 quarts (5.7L) hot water and use collected wort to dissolve extract; make to boil volume with water. Use a 2-quart (1.9L) yeast starter and mature four to eight weeks.

Notes
A more modest beer than others under this heading perhaps some would call it an Imperial porter? It's all about the specialty malts, with

good mouthfeel and nice nutty and bready notes backed up by a chocolate finish that lingers on the palate. And the name? How many Russian puns can I make?

MY TEN MOST INTERESTING RECIPES

The recipes I have given so far are all for beers that conform to our modern porter and stout guidelines. But as a result of my readings on porter, I have attempted to brew versions of eighteenth- and nineteenth-century porters and stouts that do not always fit our modern definitions, but are simply good beers in their own right. In other words, you might find it rewarding to brew one or more of them, as detailed in the first five of the following recipes. Although I have tried hard to reconstruct these beers as close to the original as possible, the new versions can never be completely authentic for a variety of reasons. Chief among these are that these old recipes are often obscure about details of the process, and that modern ingredients are different from their predecessors. This has meant that Jeff Browning and I have had to interpret old recipes in the light of our modern knowledge of brewing procedures, and of the properties of modern ingredients, in order to achieve satisfactory results. We make no apology for the fact that, as always, our main aim is to produce good beer!

The reproduction beers were all produced in my own homebrewery, and some were then scaled up to ten barrels and brewed at BrüRm@ BAR in New Haven. They are followed by five more recipes, which are not "reproductions," but are based on modern craft-brewed beers. As was the case with the earlier recipes, these are all based on a five-gallon (19L) brew length and are presented assuming a brew house efficiency of 65 percent. All of the other assumptions listed at the beginning of this chapter also apply, including 25 percent utilization of hop α-acids. Of course, the latter is based on guesswork as to what bittering levels the old beers might have had, which is something we shall never know, just as the brewers then never knew about α-acids!

1744 Porter

(all-grain)

Ingredients

12.0 lb. (5.4 kg) UK mild ale malt (4°L); 76%
1.5 lb. (680 g) Crisp brown malt (65°L); 9.5%
1.5 lb. (680 g) UK crystal malt (80°L); 9.5%
0.8 lb. (360 g) Briess BlackPrinz® malt (500°L); 5.1%
1.3 oz. (37 g) Magnum pellets, 12.4% AA (16 AAU, 90 min.)
0.5 oz. (14 g) East Kent Goldings (15 min.)
0.5 oz. (14 g) East Kent Goldings (0 min)
Wyeast 1098 Whitbread Ale

Original gravity: 1.074 (18.0°P)
Final gravity: 1.018 (4.6°P)
ABV: 7.3%
IBU: 60 (67 with contribution from late addition)
SRM: 133

Directions

Mash at 150 to 152°F (65.6 to 66.7°C) with 20 quarts (19L) water; add Magnum hops at start, first EKG at last 15 minutes, and second EKG at end of boil. Use a yeast starter of 1.5 quarts (1.4L), and mature for three to six weeks.

Notes

This recipe is one version of several I brewed based on one from the London and Country Brewer. However, that used only brown malt, which does not work with the modern version of that malt. I opted for mild ale malt (which would have been closer to the pale malt of that time) and a mix of specialty malts to approximate the flavor of the original. In particular, I went for de-bittered black malt, since high-roast malts were not known in 1744. We called it "Presumptuous Porter" in the BAR version, to reflect our feelings about what we were trying to do. It's an excellent beer, very malty and full-bodied with a plethora of other flavors, including raisin, plum, coffee, and licorice; a bottle kept fifteen years held all these flavors well, although it had developed some acidity by that time.

Extract version

Substitute 10.5 pounds (4.8 kg) of the pale malt with 7 pounds (3.2 kg) light LME syrup, and do a partial mash with the remaining 1.5 pounds (0.680 g) mild ale malt, along with the other grains.

Turn of the Century Porter

(all-grain)

Ingredients

10.0 lb. (4.5 kg) Maris Otter 2-row pale malt (4°L); 74.1%
3.5 lb. (1.59 kg) Crisp brown malt (65°L); 25.9%
2.5 oz. (71 g) East Kent Goldings pellets, 5.0% AA (12.5 AAU, 90 min.)
White Labs WLP002 English Ale

Original gravity: 1.063 (15.4°P)
Final gravity: 1.016 (4.1°P)
ABV: 6.2%
IBU: 33
SRM: 54

Directions

Mash at 150 to 152°F (65.6 to 66.7°C) with 17 quarts (16L) of water; add all hops at start of boil. Use a yeast starter of 1.5 quarts (1.4L), and mature two to four weeks.

Notes

Here we have a recipe that I think might have been similar to those brewed in London and Ireland around the late 1700s to early 1800s, when use of the hydrometer showed brewers that brown malt gave a relatively low yield of extract. The recipe is based on several sources of the time, some of which gave actual original gravities. I opted for EK

Goldings as the nearest modern equivalent, as this variety was known at this time. Since cold storage was not then practiced, I used the conservative figure of 2% AA for the original in calculating what the bitterness levels might have been.

The flavor of this rather pale porter was interesting—quite malty, some coffee notes, and plenty of licorice/anise tastes up front. Yet the beer had a disappointing finish, so when we brewed in at BrüRm@ BAR, we adjusted the above recipe by substituting 2 pounds (0.91 kg) of pale malt with 1 pound (0.454 kg) each of Briess Victory and chocolate malts. We also added 1 ounce (28 g) Columbus hops for the last thirty minutes and 1 ounce (28 g) EK Goldings at the end of the boil. That produced a much more satisfying drink, with bready, chocolate, and roasted notes, as well as some earthy, spicy hop characteristics to give a nice finish to the beer.

Amsinck No. 11 Dublin Stout

(all-grain)

Ingredients
17.0 lb. (7.7 kg) Maris Otter 2-row pale malt (4°L); 95.8%
0.75 lb. (340 g) Baird black malt (550°L); 4.2%
2.3 oz. (65 g) Target pellets, 10.0% AA (23 AAU, 90 min.)
White Labs WLP004 Irish Ale

Original gravity: 1.085 (20.3°P)
Final gravity: 1.026 (6.6°P)
ABV: 7.8%
IBU: 86
SRM: 96

Directions
Mash at 151 to 153°F (66.1 to 67.2°C) with 22 quarts (21L) of water, and add all hops at start of boil. Use a yeast starter of 1.5 quarts (1.4L), and mature for three to six weeks.

Notes

This brew is based on a nineteenth-century book (Amsinck, 1868). I throw it in here because it is a very simple recipe that reflects what an English brewer thought of as Irish stout at a time when Guinness had become the world's major brewer of stout and porter. I had to guess at the mash temperature, because the brewer only measured it at the run-off taps at the end of the mash! It drinks very much like a dry stout, quite dry with substantial bitterness from the black malt and high hop rate. Indeed, the IBU level actually puts it in the region of a modern American stout!

Extract version

Replace the pale malt with 12 pounds (5.4 kg) of pale LME syrup, and steep the black malt separately in a muslin bag with 1.5 quarts (1.4L) of water at around 160°F (71°C). Strain off and rinse grains with two lots of 1.5 quarts (1.4L) hot water and use this wort to dissolve the extract.

Barclay's Imperial Brown Stout

(all-grain)

Ingredients

13.0 lb. (5.9 kg) Maris Otter 2-row pale malt (4°L); 55.3%
3.0 lb. (1.36 kg) Crisp amber malt (29°L); 12.8%
6.5 lb. (2.95 kg) Crisp brown malt (65°L); 27.7%
1.0 lb. (454 g) Baird black malt (550°L); 4.3%
3.0 oz. (85 g) Columbus pellets, 12.0% AA (36 AAU, 90 min.)
Wyeast 1098 Whitbread Ale

Original gravity: 1.109 (25.8°P)
Final gravity: 1.040 (9.9°P)
ABV: 9.2%
IBU: 100?
SRM: 222

Directions

Mash at 150 to 151°F (65.6 to 66.1°C) with 29 quarts (27L) of water; you will probably need to sparge to collect at least 7 gallons (26.5L) and boil down to 5 gallons (19L) to obtain the target gravity. If so, add the bittering hops for the last ninety minutes of the boil. Use a starter of 3 quarts (2.8L) from three packs of yeast, and mature six months minimum.

Notes

This is my version of this beer, but another version is given by the Durden Park Beer Circle (1991). For the sake of uniformity, I have kept the brew length to 5 gallons (19L); however, because of the large quantities of malt involved, you may well find it more practical to reduce it to 3 gallons (11.4L). I have used an "unauthentic" American hop, simply because I wanted to use a high α-acid hop, so as to limit the amount of trub in the boiler. The figure of 100 IBU I give above is a calculation, and it will probably be less than that, because of limits on the solubility of iso-alpha acids in this high gravity wort.

The significance of this beer is that it was one of, if not *the* original Russian Imperial stouts, exported by Barclay to Russia from London. The recipe here gives an excellent Imperial stout, very full-bodied and chewy with background notes of toffee, licorice, roast coffee, and raisin, backed up by firm hop bitterness. I recently tried a 7-year-old sample, and it had lost nothing in the keeping!

Incidentally, we did not brew a version of this at BAR, because it was just too big a beer to cope with, with the combination of production pressures and vessel capacities. Size does matter! Equally, an extract version is not practical, because the large proportion of brown malt would mean too great a scale for a partial mash to be carried out.

Pale Porter

(all-grain)

Ingredients

17.0 lb. (7.7 kg) UK 2-row pale malt (2°L); 91.9%
1.5 lb. (0.68 kg) brown sugar as Essentia bina; 8.1%

2.0 oz. (57 g) Columbus pellets, 12.0% AA (24 AAU, 90 min.)
White Labs WLP004 Irish Ale

Original gravity: 1.082 (19.8°P)*
Final gravity: 1.018 (4.6°P)
ABV: 8.5%
IBU: 90
SRM: 37

Directions

Prepare the essentia bina as follows:

Take the sugar (use the darkest form you can find) and dissolve it up with about ¼ pint of water in a shallow saucepan; boil the mixture until it starts to caramelize and bubble. Continue heating until a sample taken solidifies immediately when placed on the back of a cold spoon, and turn the heat off. Immediately add ½ pint of cold water, stirring vigorously so the whole mixture takes on the consistency of a syrup, adding more cold water if necessary. Note that Joseph Coppinger (1815) recommends setting fire to the mixture as the heat is turned off, and allowing it to burn for several minutes, and I have seen similar suggestions in several English references. You can try this if you want to; I did not, as I have seen how quickly sugar can burn, and I did not want a fire in my kitchen! I had no way to determine what the color of my essentia bina was, so the numbers given above are a pure guess, in which I assumed 100°L for it (by visual examination). *Note that the OG may be a little higher than I have given, depending upon how far you have taken the caramelization of the essentia bina.

Mash at 152 to 154°F (66.7 to 67.8°C) with 21 quarts (20L) of water; add all hops at the start and the essentia at the end of the wort boil. Use a yeast starter of 2 quarts (1.9L) from two packs of yeast, and mature three to six weeks.

Notes

This is here for a couple of reasons, the first being that it comes from a book published for Americans in America in 1815. The author, Joseph Coppinger, was an Englishman, but had lived in America for some years. It is not clear whether he actually brewed in the United States, however, and he makes a plea for the "citizens of the town" to set up a brewery, presumably in New York, as that was where the book was published. The second reason is that it cites the use of essentia bina, or porter coloring. This enabled him to offer a recipe for a beer based only on pale malt, and using no brown or porter malt at all. But do note that Coppinger referred to essentia bina as also being made from molasses, which would have been a very American approach, although he stated that using molasses gave a product inferior to that made from Muscovado sugar.

What of the beer itself? Well, my version was not the best beer I have ever drunk, although it was quite pleasant. Despite the numbers I have estimated for color above, this was relatively light-colored for a porter, although still with a nice warming red hue to it. It was quite malty, with some roasted/burnt notes from the essentia bina, and backed with very definite hop bitterness. Which leaves open the question as to how it might have tasted if I hadn't been too much of a wimp to set my caramelized sugar alight, doesn't it?

Big Wood Porter

(all-grain)

Ingredients

9.0 lb. (4.1 kg) Briess Ashburne® mild ale malt (5°L); 65.5%

2.75 lb. (1.25 kg) Crisp brown malt (65°L); 20%

0.5 lb. (227 g) Simpson chocolate malt (410°L); 3.6%

1.0 lb. (454 g) Briess BlackPrinz® malt (500°L); 7.3%

0.5 lb. (227 g) rolled oats (3°L); 3.6%

1.4 oz. (40 g) Northern Brewer pellets, 8.5% AA (12 AAU, 90 min.)

0.5 oz. (14 g) East Kent Goldings pellets, 5.0% AA (30 min.)

1.0 oz. (28 g) East Kent Goldings pellets, 5.0% AA (0 min.)

White Labs WLP002 English Ale

Original gravity: 1.064 (15.7°P)
Final gravity: 1.016 (4.1°P)
ABV: 6.3%
IBU: 45 (58 with contribution from late additions)
SRM: 186

Directions

Mash at 150 to 152°F (65.6 to 66.7°C) with 17 quarts (16L), add Northern Brewer hops at start, first portion of Goldings at thirty minutes before, and second portion at end of boil; mature two to four weeks.

Notes

This is not a re-creation from the past, but an American beer brewed at BrüRm@BAR and designed by assistant brewer and fireman Dave Wood (hence the title). Dave thinks of it as being a porter, but it could be described as an oatmeal stout also. I prefer to call it a brown porter, because the black malt flavors are quite soft and not harsh, so that it has only background roast flavor, with chocolate and coffee hints and a malty licorice character up front, together with slight spiciness from the late-added Goldings hops.

Russian Émigré Imperial Stout

(all-grain)

Ingredients

12 lb. (4.3 kg) US 2-row pale malt (2°L); 55.8%
2.0 lb. (0.91 kg) Briess Munich malt (10°L); 9.3%
2.0 lb. (0.91 kg) Briess rye malt (4°L); 9.3%
2.0 lb. (0.91 kg) Fawcett crystal rye malt (75°L); 9.3%
2.0 lb. (0.91 kg) Briess Cara Brown® malt (55°L); 9.3%
1.5 lb. (0.68 kg) Fawcett pale chocolate malt (200°L); 7%
1.5 oz. (42 g) Magnum pellets, 14% AA (21 AAU, 90 min.)
White Labs WLP007 Dry English Ale

Original gravity: 1.101 (23.9°P)
Final gravity: 1.020 (5.1°P)
ABV: 10.8%
IBU: 78
SRM: 122

Directions

Mash at 150 to 152°F (65.6 to 66.7°C) with 27 quarts (26L) of water. You will need to sparge to collect 7 to 8 gallons (26 to 30L) of wort, and boil down to 5 gallons in order to achieve target gravity. Add the hops only for the last ninety minutes of the boil. Use a starter of at least 3 quarts (2.8L) made from three packs of yeast, and preferably to oxygenate the wort before pitching the yeast. Mature three to six months.

Notes

This is my homage to Igor Sikorsky, the helicopter manufacturer whose factory sits at the bottom of the hill at the top of which I live. It was inspired by Stratford's new commercial enterprise, Two Roads Brewing, and their Imperial stout, Igor's Dream. It is not a match for their recipe (Phil Markowski wouldn't give it to me!), but is simply something I put together after tasting the beer. Phil did emphasize the rye character of their beer, which was enhanced by aging it in rye whiskey barrels. That may not be practical for you, unless you want to experiment by adding a little (very little!) rye whiskey to your beer. A key to this beer is good attenuation, because it should definitely not finish sweet, or the rye malt spiciness will not come through on the palate. For that reason, I went for a low roast chocolate and no black malt in the grist, so the roast flavors sit in the background and do not dominate everything else.

BAR Dam' Good Stout

(all-grain)

Ingredients

9.0 lb. (4.1 kg) US 2-row pale malt (2°L); 67.2%
1.0 lb. (454 g) UK crystal malt (75°L); 7.5%

1.0 lb. (454 g) Crisp brown malt (65°L); 7.5%
1.0 lb. (454 g) Simpson black malt (550°L); 7.5%
1.0 lb. (454 g) Simpson roasted barley (550°L); 7.5%
0.4 lb. (180 g) flaked barley (1.5°L)
0.75 oz. (21 g) Northern Brewer pellets, 7.8%AA (5.9 AAU, 90 min.)
1.0 oz. (28 g) Mount Hood pellets, 6% AA (0 min.)
1.0 oz. (28 g) Willamette pellets, 4% AA (0 min.)
White Labs WLP002 English Ale

Original gravity: 1.063 (15.4°P)
Final gravity: 1.019 (4.8°P)
ABV: 5.7%
IBU: 22 (37 with contribution from late additions)
SRM: 252

Directions
Mash at 150 to 153°F (65.6 to 67.2°C) using 17 quarts (16L) of water; use a 2-quart (1.9L) yeast starter. Mature for three to six weeks.

Notes
This is part of the standard range at BrüRm@BAR, and has been so for over ten years, although we tweaked it a few years back with the introduction of brown malt to the grist. It appears to be an American stout from the use of flavoring hops, but is relatively low in bitterness for that style. Though it has definite roasted character from the black malt and roasted barley, this is somewhat modified by the licorice character of the brown malt and the caramel flavor from the crystal malt, so that roasted notes do not dominate this beer. The overall result is very well-balanced, smooth, and very drinkable; it rivals the best of IPAs as a "go-to beer" in my book!

Extract version
Substitute 5 pounds (2.3 kg) pale LME syrup for 7.5 pounds (3.4 kg) pale malt, and use the remaining 1.5 pounds (680 g) to do a partial mash at 150 to 153°F (65.6 to 7.2°C) with the rest of the grains listed above, using 7 quarts (6.6L) of water. Collect the wort, rinse the grains

with two lots of 7 quarts (6.6L), and dissolve the extract in the wort. Boil for sixty minutes, adding Northern Brewer hops at start, and Mt. Hood and Willamette hops at end of boil. Use yeast starter as above.

I know this is a big partial mash, but if you can handle it, you will find the resulting beer very enjoyable.

Anchors Aweigh!

(all-grain)

Ingredients
9.5 lb. (4.3 kg) US 2-row pale malt (2°L); 80.9%
1.0 lb. (454 g) Briess caramel malt (80°L); 8.5%
0.75 lb. (340 g) Simpson chocolate malt (410°L); 6.4%
0.5 lb. (227 g) Simpson black malt (550°L); 4.3%
1.1 oz. (31 g) Northern Brewer pellets, 8.5% AA (9.4 AAU, 90 min.)
White Labs WLP 1332 Northwest Ale

Original gravity: 1.056 (13.8°P)
Final gravity: 1.013 (3.3°P)
ABV: 5.6%
IBU: 35
SRM: 136

Directions
Mash at 150°F (65.6°C) using 14 quarts (13L) of water; add all the hops at start of boil. Use a 1-quart (1L) yeast starter; mature two to four weeks.

Notes
This is entirely my recipe, but it is a nod to Anchor Porter, which was first brewed in 1972 and is therefore one of the first porters of the new microbrewing age, although strictly speaking, Anchor was not a new brewery as such. The recipe is not intended to produce a clone of Anchor Porter, the grain bill merely being my guess as to what

would produce a smooth-tasting, roasty, and warming beer similar to Anchor's version.

Extract version

Substitute 6 pounds (2.3 kg) pale LME syrup for the pale malt above and steep the caramel, chocolate, and black malts in a muslin bag with 3 quarts (2.8L) of water at around 160°F (71°C). Strain off rinse grains with two lots of 3 quarts (2.8L) hot water and use this wort to dissolve the extract before boiling.

Pre-Prohibition Porter

(all-grain)

Ingredients

9.5 lb. (4.3 kg) US 2-row pale malt (2°L); 76.4%
0.625 lb. (280 g) Weyermann CARAFA III malt (520°L); 5%
0.625 lb. (280 g) Briess 2-row chocolate malt (350°L); 5%
0.19 lb. (86 g) Briess black malt (500°L); 1.5%
0.625 lb. (280 g) Briess flaked oats (2.5°L); 5%
0.625 lb. (280 g) Belgian Biscuit malt (25°L); 5%
0.25 lb. (113 g) Briess Smoked malt (5°L); 2%
0.5 oz. (14 g) Magnum pellets, 13.1% AA (6.6 AAU, 90 min.)
1.0 oz. (28 g) Cluster pellets, 6.5% AA (30 min.)
White Labs WLP 008 East Coast Ale

Original gravity: 1.059 (14.5°P)
Final gravity: 1.014 (3.6°P)
ABV: 5.9%
IBU: 40
SRM: 135

Directions

Mash at 148 to 150°F (64.4 to 65.6°C), with 16 quarts (15L) of water; use a 2-quart (1.9L) yeast starter. Mature two to four weeks.

Notes

This is an adaptation of a recipe kindly provided by David Wollner, the owner of Willimantic Brewing in Willimantic, Connecticut. The building housing David's Main Street Café dated to before Prohibition, so he thought it appropriate to celebrate the eightieth anniversary of the repeal by putting together this brew. It's a good one, too, very full-flavored, nutty, chocolaty, just a little roasty, and very satisfying. There is also just a hint of smoke in the background on the palate, just to add a little hint of authenticity. David included Cluster hops, since they would almost certainly have been used in pre-Prohibition porters. Note that the IBU number I have given is based on a significant contribution from the Clusters.

Dave Wollner at his Main Street Café, Willimantic, Connecticut.

ADDENDUM TO RECIPES

1. CARBONATION

Many published recipes (including some of mine!) give recommendations for the amount of priming sugar to be added to a brew at kegging or bottling. It may not have escaped your notice that I have not done so in the recipes given in this direction. That is partly because I tend to like a lower carbonation level than do most American drinkers, and I don't want to talk you out of doing it your way! But also, it is nearly impossible to recommend precise amounts of priming sugar, since there is always some residual CO_2 no matter how flat the beer looks to be, and you never know just how much CO_2 you have present when you are ready to put the beer into its last container. That is because CO_2 equilibrium pressure in beer varies with temperature, so that the level of gas in the beer depends on the fermentation and storage temperatures employed.

2. KEGGING

That does not matter if you are kegging, since in this case you do not need to prime at all, and can just force-carbonate the beer with your gas cylinder. Let's assume that you are looking for a gas content of 2 to 2.5 volumes in your porter or stout, which is where most of you will want to be. I recommend that these beers should be drunk at no lower than 40 to 45°F (4.4 to 7.2°C), and you are probably not going to want it any warmer than that. This means that you will want to apply a CO_2 pressure of 10 to 12 psig. So when the beer has been racked into the keg and the latter has been sealed, set your gas pressure gauge at this pressure and open the gas valve. In two to five days, the gas level in the beer should have reached equilibrium with the applied pressure, and the beer is ready to dispense and drink. Some brewers apply a higher pressure and then vigorously shake the keg for some time before reducing the pressure back to the desired serving level. This is based on the idea that the surface area of the beer exposed to the applied gas is greatly increased, and the rate of dissolution of the gas is increased. It is possible to "over gas" the beer this way if you apply too much excess pressure and shake for too long, so I prefer to be patient and just leave the keg alone at the desired pressure for a few days.

Note that if you want to serve your beer at a more "British" temperature of 50°F (10°C), you would need an applied pressure of 10 to 13 psig to achieve around 2 volumes CO_2 in the beer. At 55°F (12.8°C), which is the top end of what might be expected in a good English pub cellar, you would need a pressure of 13 to 14 psig in order to reach the same carbonation level. To get up to 2.5 volumes CO_2 at these temperatures you would need to raise the pressure to 17 to 20 psig. For further information, there are various published charts, especially on the Internet, showing values for volumes of CO_2 as a function of temperature and pressure (see, for example, the first reference I pulled off the web: www.kegerators.com/articles/carbonation).

3. BOTTLING

This is somewhat trickier, as you don't know quite how much gas is present in your beer when you rack it. You can make a good guess if you keep the green beer at a steady temperature during secondary fermentation. This is easy enough if you possess a stainless conical fermenter equipped with a thermometer, such as are now available from homebrewing suppliers. However, these are expensive, and if you have one, you probably also have a kegging system and can proceed as in the preceding paragraphs. So let's assume you use a glass secondary fermenter, and that the beer has remained at 65 to 70°F (18.3 to 21.1°C). The pressure-temperature chart tells us that the beer will contain about 0.7 to 0.9 volumes of CO_2 (but remember that this chart is about equilibrium conditions, which will not apply if the beer temperature has risen and then fallen during the secondary).

So, to achieve 2.0 to 2.5 volumes CO_2, you need to "add" 1.3 to 1.5 volumes of gas in the form of priming sugar. Now, 1 ounce of glucose in 5 gallons (19L) of beer will give 0.37 volumes of CO_2 (take my word for it!), so you will need to prime with 3.5 to 4.1 ounces (99 to 125 g) of glucose in order to reach our carbonation target. But this is for anhydrous glucose, and what most homebrewers use is corn sugar, which is glucose monohydrate. Therefore, you need to add about 10 percent more of this than for the anhydrous material; in our case, that means we need 3.9 to 4.5 ounces (110 to 128 g) of corn sugar. If you prefer to use cane, rather than corn sugar, you will require an equivalent amount, except that this is not hydrated. So, to a close approximation, use the original numbers of 3.5 to 4.1 ounces (99 to 125 g) of cane sugar.

Of course, if you have done a cold fermentation, such as with Baltic porter brewed with lager yeast, the situation is a little different. If you have carried out a true lager stage at, say, 35°F (1.7°C), you will have around 1.5 volumes of CO_2 in the beer. So you need a further 1 volume to reach a target of 2.5 volumes, and that requires 2.7 ounces (76 g) of anhydrous glucose, or 3 ounces (85 g) of corn sugar. That assumes you have not done a diacetyl rest at 65 to 70°F (18 to 21°C); if you have, then proceed as instructed in the preceding paragraph.

This is just a brief guide to priming; you might want to consult a more specialist account of this procedure, or you might just want to continue adding the same amount of priming sugar as you have always done! What I have tried to point out is that a beer that has finished fermenting may appear flat, but can still have a significant amount of carbonation. Ignoring that fact and priming as though the beer is truly flat at that stage is a very good way to soak your carpet every time you open a bottle of it!

4. STOUT DISPENSE AND NITROGEN GAS

Guinness has done a great job of marketing over the years, and perhaps their biggest achievement was to convince stout drinkers that their nitrogen-based method of dispensing was the only true method for serving their black gold. I think it has perhaps been somewhat over-rated, yet I must confess that on occasion, I too have been mesmerized by that deep explosion of tiny bubbles in the body of the beer, finally settling out to that very fine and distinctively dense head. Yet there is more than just an aesthetic effect here, because this technique results in a relatively low-carbonated beer, containing not much above 1 volume of CO_2. This is good, because dry stout has a tendency towards an acid flavor, which could be quite unpleasant if the beer was more highly carbonated.

How do they do this? Well, the first part of the answer is that they use a special type of dispense faucet. The second part is that the beer is dispensed by means of a nitrogen/carbon dioxide mix, rather than the latter alone. Special stout faucets like these are widely available, although they are relatively expensive at around $80. But you will also need the mixed gas, for you can't use CO_2 alone to drive the beer through the faucet. That is because the faucet contains a restrictor plate that slows the flow of beer through tiny perforations, which is what causes the production of those tiny bubbles. As a result, you need a gas pressure on the keg of around 30 psig to get a reasonable flow of beer, and that would mean that the beer would be way over-carbonated using CO_2 alone. This does not happen with the mixed gas (usually 75 percent nitrogen, 25 percent carbon dioxide) because the presence of the nitrogen limits the solubility of the CO_2. The nitrogen itself has very limited solubility in beer, and bursts out as tiny bubbles when the beer is forced through the restrictor. The shear forces applied by the restrictor plate mean the bubbles formed are quite uniform, and so form a stable head that does not easily collapse into larger bubbles. This gas mixture is available from some homebrew suppliers, and should also be obtainable from local gas suppliers. They are not particularly cheap; a cylinder will cost around $90, and a regulator (different from those used for CO_2) about $70.

Since stouts are normally fermented at around 65 to 70°F (18.3 to 21.1°C), as noted above, the beer will contain about 0.8 volumes of beer when kegging. That means that priming with 1 ounce (28 g) of glucose will take it up nicely to around 1.1 to 1.2 volumes of CO_2, just right if you want to dispense the beer directly by pushing it out with mixed gas. But many brewers consider it best to allow some equilibration between the gas and the beer. You can do this as described above by setting the regulator to 30 psig and opening the valve to the keg (which is at your desired serving temperature), then leaving the gas on for a week or so until equilibrium is reached. Commercial breweries often use a carbonation stone and bubble the gas through this into the beer for thirty minutes to an hour or so.

At BrüRm@Bar, we dispense all our beers (including our stout) with mixed gas, after having brought them to the desired CO_2 level by capping the fermenter at an appropriate stage towards the end of fermentation. In this case, the mixed gas really just pushes the beer, rather than coming to equilibrium with it, yet it does permit the formation of a tight head on the stout. What I am really saying is that this is what suits us (and our drinkers), and that is exactly what you should do in deciding how you are going to dispense your stouts and porters.

Three for one: Jeff Browning, Dave Wollner, and myself in the brewery at Willimantic's Main Street Café.

SELECTED BIBLIOGRAPHY

THERE HAS BEEN MUCH WRITTEN ABOUT PORTER AND STOUT in the centuries since it was first brewed, so I felt that this list should only include the more important texts on these beers. It includes those English books, both ancient and modern, which deal with both the history of these styles and the methods of brewing them. Irish brewers had a great deal of influence in how porter and stout developed, so I found it essential to include books dealing with the major Irish brewing companies. Porters and stouts are sometimes viewed as being only British beers but they also played important roles in the American brewing industry, so I have included a number of American books dealing with both the history of brewing in the United States and porter and stout brewing procedures.

Amsinck, G. S. 1868. *Practical Brewings: a series of fifty brewings in extenso*. G. S. Amsinck.

Anonymous. 1903. *One Hundred Years of Brewing*. H. S. Rich & Co., New York; Reprint 1974 by Arno Press.

Anonymous. 1734, 1735, 1736, 1737, 1740, 1742, 1744, 1750, 1759. *The London and Country Brewer*. Various publishers.

Baron, Stanley A. 1962. *Brewing in America*. Little Brown; Reprint Edition 1998 by Ayer Co., N. Stratford, New Hampshire.

Black, W. 1849. *A Practical Treatise on Brewing*, Second edition. Smith, Elder, London.

Brande, W. 1830. *Town and Country Brewery Book*. Dean and Munday; Reprint edition 2003 by Raudins Publishing.

Byrn, M. L. 1852. *Complete Practical Brewer*. Henry Carey Baird; Reprint edition 2002 by Raudins Publishing.

Coppinger, Joseph. 1815. *The American Practical Brewer and Tanner*. Van Winkle and Riley, New York; Reprint Edition 2007 by Beer-Books.com, Cleveland, Ohio.

Cornell, Martyn. 2003. *Beer: The Story of the Pint*. Headline Book Publishing, London.

Cornell, Martyn. 2008. *Amber, Gold and Black: The History of Britain's Great Beers*. Middlesex UK, Zythography Press.

Corran, H. S. 1975. *A History of Brewing*. David and Charles, Newton Abbot, Devon.

O Drisceoil, D. and O Drisceoil, D. 1997. *The Murphy's Story*. Murphy Brewery, Ireland.

Ellis, William. 1750. *The Country Housewife's Family Companion*. Reprint edition 2000 by Prospect Books.

Foster, Terence. 1992. *Porter*. Brewers Publications, Boulder, Colorado.

Gourvish, T. R. and Wilson, R. G. 1994. *The British Brewing Industry 1830–1980*. Cambridge University Press.

Harris, John and the Durden Park Beer Circle. 1991. *Old British Beers and How to Make Them*. 2nd edition.

Hughes, D. 2006. *A Bottle of Guinness please*. Phimboy, Wokingham, Berkshire.

Jackson, M. 1988. *The New World Guide to Beer*. Running Press, Philadelphia, Pennsylvania.

Knoblock, G. A. and Gunter, J. T. 2004. *Brewing in New Hampshire*. Arcadia Publishing, Portsmouth, New Hampshire.

Lewis, Michael J. 1995. *Stout*. Brewers Publications, Boulder, Colorado.

Mathias, P. 1959. *The Brewing Industry in England 1700–1830*. Cambridge University Press. Reprint Edition 1993 by Gregg Revivals, Aldershot, Hampshire.

Noon, Mark A. 2005. *Yuengling*. McFarland and Co., Jefferson, North Carolina.

Pattinson, R. 2010. *Porter*. Kilderkin, Amsterdam (http:/www.lulu.com/shop/ronpattinson)

Pattinson, R. barclayperkins.blogspot.com (blog)

Ritchie, B. 1992. *An Uncommon Brewer, the Story of Whitbread 1742-1992*. James and James, London.

Smith, G. 1998. *Beer in America*. Brewers Publications, Boulder, Colorado.

Tizard, W. L. 1846. *The Theory and Practice of Brewing Illustrated*, second edition, W. L. Tizard, London.

Van Wieren, D. P. 1995. *American Breweries II*. Eastern Coast Breweriana Association, West Point, Pennsvylania.

Wahl, R. and Henius, M. 1908. *American Handy Book of the Brewing, Malting and Auxiliary Trades*, Volumes I and II. Wahl-Henius Institute, Chicago, Illinois.